CW01151806

Lecture Notes in Educational Technology

Series editors

Ronghuai Huang, Smart Learning Institute, Beijing Normal University, Beijing, China
Kinshuk, College of Information, University of North Texas, Denton, TX, USA
Mohamed Jemni, University of Tunis, Tunis, Tunisia
Nian-Shing Chen, Department of Information Management, National Sun Yat-sen University, Kaohsiung, Taiwan
J. Michael Spector, University of North Texas, Denton, TX, USA

Lecture Notes in Educational Technology

The series *Lecture Notes in Educational Technology* (LNET), has established itself as a medium for the publication of new developments in the research and practice of educational policy, pedagogy, learning science, learning environment, learning resources etc. in information and knowledge age, – quickly, informally, and at a high level.

More information about this series at http://www.springer.com/series/11777

Maiga Chang · Elvira Popescu
Kinshuk · Nian-Shing Chen
Mohamed Jemni · Ronghuai Huang
J. Michael Spector
Editors

Challenges and Solutions in Smart Learning

Proceeding of 2018 International Conference on Smart Learning Environments, Beijing, China

Springer

Editors
Maiga Chang
Athabasca University
Edmonton, AB
Canada

Elvira Popescu
University of Craiova
Craiova
Romania

Kinshuk
College of Information
University of North Texas
Denton, TX
USA

Nian-Shing Chen
National Sun Yat-sen University
Kaohsiung
Taiwan

Mohamed Jemni
Computer Science and Educational
  Technologies
University of Tunis
Tunis
Tunisia

Ronghuai Huang
Smart Learning Institute
Beijing Normal University
Beijing
China

J. Michael Spector
University of North Texas
Denton, TX
USA

ISSN 2196-4963   ISSN 2196-4971 (electronic)
Lecture Notes in Educational Technology
ISBN 978-981-10-8742-4   ISBN 978-981-10-8743-1 (eBook)
https://doi.org/10.1007/978-981-10-8743-1

Library of Congress Control Number: 2018934926

© Springer Nature Singapore Pte Ltd. 2018
This work is subject to copyright. All rights are reserved by the Publisher, whether the whole or part of the material is concerned, specifically the rights of translation, reprinting, reuse of illustrations, recitation, broadcasting, reproduction on microfilms or in any other physical way, and transmission or information storage and retrieval, electronic adaptation, computer software, or by similar or dissimilar methodology now known or hereafter developed.
The use of general descriptive names, registered names, trademarks, service marks, etc. in this publication does not imply, even in the absence of a specific statement, that such names are exempt from the relevant protective laws and regulations and therefore free for general use.
The publisher, the authors and the editors are safe to assume that the advice and information in this book are believed to be true and accurate at the date of publication. Neither the publisher nor the authors or the editors give a warranty, express or implied, with respect to the material contained herein or for any errors or omissions that may have been made. The publisher remains neutral with regard to jurisdictional claims in published maps and institutional affiliations.

Printed on acid-free paper

This Springer imprint is published by the registered company Springer Nature Singapore Pte Ltd. part of Springer Nature
The registered company address is: 152 Beach Road, #21-01/04 Gateway East, Singapore 189721, Singapore

Preface

Smart learning environments are emerging as an offshoot of various technology-enhanced learning initiatives that have aimed over the years at improving learning experiences and outcomes by making learning more efficient through creating learning space and atmosphere that meet the individual needs of learners, while still enabling learners to access digital resources and interact with learning systems at the place and time of their choice.

The concept of what constitutes smart learning is still in its infancy, and the International Conference on Smart Learning Environments (ICSLE) is organized by the International Association on Smart Learning Environments and has emerged as the platform to bring together researchers, practitioners, and policy makers to discuss issues related to the optimization of learning environments to enhance learning. The focus is on the interplay of pedagogy, content knowledge, technology and their interactions and interdepencies towards the advancement of smart learning environments.

ICSLE will facilitate opportunities for discussions and constructive dialogue among various stakeholders on the limitations of existing learning environments, need for reform, innovative uses of emerging pedagogical approaches and technologies, and sharing and promotion of best practices, leading to the evolution, design and implementation of smart learning environments.

The focus of the contributions in this book is on the challenges and solutions in smart learning and smart learning environments that researchers have faced and proposed. Various components of this book include but are not limited to:

- Assessment and gamification in smart learning environments
- Innovative uses of emerging and existing technologies
- Learning analytics, technologies and tools to support smart learning environments.

ICSLE 2018 received 27 papers, with authors from 11 countries. All submissions were peer-reviewed in a double-blind review process by at least 3 Program Committee members. We are pleased to note that the quality of the submissions this year turned out to be very high. A total of 7 papers were accepted as full papers (yielding a 25.93% acceptance rate). In addition, 5 papers were selected for presentation as short papers and another 4 as posters.

Furthermore, ICSLE 2018 features joint activities with US-China Smart Education Conference and presents 5 distinguished keynote presentations. A Smart Computing and Intelligence Summit is also included in the program. One workshop is also organized in conjunction with the main conference, with a total of 3 accepted papers (included at the end of this volume).

We acknowledge the invaluable assistance of the 42 Program Committee members from 22 countries, who provided timely and helpful reviews. We would also like to thank the entire Organizing Committee for their efforts and time spent to ensure the success of the conference. And last but not least, we would like to thank all the authors for their contribution in maintaining a high quality conference.

With all the effort that has gone into the process, by authors and reviewers, we are confident that this year's ICSLE proceedings will immediately earn a place as an indispensable overview of the state of the art and will have significant archival value in the longer term.

Edmonton, Canada	Maiga Chang
Craiova, Romania	Elvira Popescu
Denton, USA	Kinshuk
Kaohsiung, Taiwan	Nian-Shing Chen
Tunis, Tunisia	Mohamed Jemni
Beijing, China	Ronghuai Huang
Denton, USA	J. Michael Spector
January 2018	

Chairs/Committees

Conference Chairs
- **Dong Qi**, Beijing Normal University, China
- **Neal Smatresk**, University of North Texas, USA

Honorary Chairs
- **Larry Johnson**, EdFutures.org, USA
- **Diana Laurillard**, Institute of Education, UK
- **Demetrios G. Sampson**, Curtin University, Australia

General Chairs
- **Kinshuk**, College of Information, University of North Texas, Denton, TX, USA
- **Nian-Shing Chen**, National Sun Yat-sen University, Taiwan
- **Mohamed Jemni**, ALECSO, Tunisia

Program Chairs
- **Maiga Chang**, Athabasca University, Canada
- **Elvira Popescu**, University of Craiova, Romania

Local Chairs
- **Ronghuai Huang**, Beijing Normal University, China
- **J. Michael Spector**, The University of North Texas, USA

Workshop/Panel Chairs
- **Vive Kumar**, Athabasca University, Canada
- **Ting-Wen Chang**, Beijing Normal University, China

Publicity Chairs
- **Guang Chen**, Beijing Normal University, China
- **Michail N. Giannakos**, Norwegian University of Science and Technology, Norway
- **Isabelle Guillot**, Athabasca University, Canada

Technical Operations Chairs
- **Rébecca Guillot**, Athabasca University, Canada
- **Richard Tortorella**, University of Eastern Finland, Finland
- **Marc Denojean-Mairet**, ByteForce Media, Canada
- **Junfeng Yang**, Hangzhou Normal University, China

International Scientific Committee
- **Marie-Helene Abel**, Université de Technologie de Compiègne, France
- **Diana Andone**, Politehnica University of Timisoara, Romania
- **Jorge Luis Bacca Acosta**, University of Girona, Spain
- **Su Cai**, Faculty of Education, Beijing Normal University, China
- **Wei Cheng**, Beijing Normal University, China
- **Feng-Kuang Chiang**, Shanghai Normal University, China
- **Maria-Iuliana Dascalu**, University Politehnica of Bucharest, Romania
- **Mihai Dascalu**, University Politehnica of Bucharest, Romania
- **Stavros Demetriadis**, Aristotle University of Thessaloniki, Greece
- **Michael Derntl**, University of Tübingen, Germany
- **Giuliana Dettori**, Istituto di Tecnologie Didattiche del CNR, Italy
- **Panagiotis Germanakos**, SAP SE & University of Cyprus, Cyprus
- **Chaohua Gong**, Southwest University, China
- **Gabriela Grosseck**, University of the West Timisoara, Romania
- **Isabelle Guillot**, Athabasca Universty, Canada
- **Tsukasa Hirashima**, Hiroshima University, Japan
- **Carmen Holotescu**, Timsoft, Romania
- **Gwo-Jen Hwang**, National Taiwan University, Taiwan
- **Hazra Imran**, The University of British Columbia, Canada
- **Malinka Ivanova**, Technical University of Sofia, Bulgaria
- **Mirjana Ivanovic**, University of Novi Sad, Serbia
- **Mohamed Koutheaïr Khribi**, Latice, Tunisia
- **Tomaž Klobučar**, Jozef Stefan Institute, Slovenia
- **Siu Cheung Kong**, The Education University of Hong Kong, Hong Kong
- **Vivekanandan Kumar**, Athabasca University, Canada
- **Rita Kuo**, New Mexico Institute of Mining and Technology, USA
- **George Magoulas**, Birkbeck College, UK
- **Katherine Maillet**, Institut Mines-Télécom, France
- **Ivana Marenzi**, L3S Research Center, Germany

- **Alke Martens**, University of Rostock, Germany
- **Sahana Murthy**, Indian Institute of Technology Bombay, India
- **Alexandros Paramythis**, Contexity AG, Switzerland
- **Demetrios Sampson**, Curtin University, Australia
- **Masanori Sugimoto**, Hokkaido University, Japan
- **Vincent Tam**, The University of Hong Kong, Hong Kong
- **Marco Temperini**, Sapienza University of Rome, Italy
- **Carlos Vaz de Carvalho**, GILT-ISEP, Portugal
- **Riina Vuorikari**, Institute for Prospective Technological Studies (IPTS), Spain
- **Minhong Wang**, The University of Hong Kong, Hong Kong
- **Junfeng Yang**, Hangzhou Normal University, China
- **Jinbao Zhang**, Beijing Normal University, China
- **Lanqin Zheng**, Beijing Normal University, China

Tutorial: Is Educational Research a Matter of Digital Observations and Data Balancing?

Presenters
- **Shawn Fraser**, Athabasca University, Canada
- **David Boulanger**, Athabasca University, Canada
- **Vive Kumar**, Athabasca University, Canada

2nd International Workshop on Technologies Assist Teaching and Administration (TATA 2018)

Workshop Organizer
- **Maiga Chang**, Athabasca University, Canada

Contents

Part I Main Conference Papers

A Gamified Approach to Automated Assessment of Programming Assignments... 3
Giuseppina Polito and Marco Temperini

A Smart Learning Environment for Environmental Education....... 13
Ilkka Jormanainen, Tapani Toivonen and Ville Nivalainen

An interdisciplinary Framework for Designing Smart Learning Environments... 17
Sirkka Freigang, Lars Schlenker and Thomas Köhler

Application Development on Tablet to Promote a Classroom Research Skills for SSRU' Students.................................. 21
Chaiwat Waree

Constructing a Smart Chinese International Learning Environment Based on Learning Analytics Technology....................... 25
Juan Xu, Yanlan Shi and Yongbin Zhou

Effects of Reciprocal Feedback on EFL Learners' Communication Strategy Use and Oral Communicative Performance............... 31
Sie Wai Chew, Wei-Chieh Fang, Chia-Ning Hsu and Nian-Shing Chen

Exploring General Morphological Analysis and Providing Personalized Recommendations to Stimulate Creativity with *ReaderBench*... 41
Daniela Stamati, Maria-Dorinela Sirbu, Mihai Dascalu and Stefan Trausan-Matu

Higher Cognitive Items Generation Algorithms 51
Ebenezer Aggrey, Maiga Chang, Rita Kuo and Xiaokun Zhang

Innovative Maker Movement Platform for K-12 Education as a Smart Learning Environment 61
Tapani Toivonen, Ilkka Jormanainen, Calkin Suero Montero and Andrea Alessandrini

Smart Interactions for the Quantified Self 67
Erik Isaksson and Björn Hedin

Smart watches for making EFL learning effective, healthy, and happy 73
Rustam Shadiev, Wu-Yuin Hwang, Narzikul Shadiev, Mirzaali Fayziev, Tzu-Yu Liu and Lingjie Shen

StudentViz: A Tool for Visualizing Students' Collaborations in a Social Learning Environment 77
Alex Becheru, Andreea Calota and Elvira Popescu

The *Edutainment* Platform: Interactive Storytelling Relying on Semantic Similarity 87
Irina Toma, Florentina Bacioiu, Mihai Dascalu and Stefan Trausan-Matu

The effects of student interaction with blog-based course content on learning performance 97
Benazir Quadir, Jie Chi Yang, Jun Zhang and Houli Gao

The *Objective Ear*: Assessing the Progress of a Music Task 107
Joel Burrows and Vivekanandan Kumar

Visualizing and Understanding Information literacy Research Based on the CiteSpaceV 113
Liqin Yu, Di Wu, Sha Zhu and Huan Li

Part II Tutorial: Is Educational Research a Matter of Digital Observations and Data Balancing?

Open Research and Observational Study for 21st Century Learning.. 121
Vivekanandan S. Kumar, Shawn Fraser and David Boulanger

Part III 2nd International Workshop on Technologies Assisting Teaching and Administration

An educational role-playing game for modeling the learner's personality 129
Mouna Denden, Ahmed Tlili, Fathi Essalmi and Mohamed Jemni

Annotation Recommendation for Online Reading Activities 135
Miao-Han Chang, Maiga Chang, Rita Kuo, Fathi Essalmi,
Vivekanandan S. Kumar and Hsu-Yang Kung

**Big Data Analytics and Smart Service Tool: "Smart Learning
Partner" Platform** 141
Xiaoqing Li, Linghong Du and Xuanwei Ma

Part I
Main Conference Papers

A Gamified Approach to Automated Assessment of Programming Assignments

Giuseppina Polito, and Marco Temperini

Dept. of Computer, Control, and Management Engineering
Sapienza University, Rome, Italy
marte@diag.uniroma1.it, joypolito@hotmail.it

Abstract. Tools delivering assessment, and feedback, for students' programming assignments are important in computer science education. Approaches range from the static analysis of program correctness, to testing-based evaluation, through the application in frameworks of competitive programming. In this paper we describe a testing-based approach, provided in a gamified web-based environment. Students provide their solutions to assignments; such solutions are tested and graded, and their quality contributes to the contents of the student's profile, where experience points, medals on assignments, assignment categories badges, and overall status allow students to monitor their achievements and have engagement and motivation increasing. Being at this time not possible a formal experimentation of the system, we provide an analysis of its actual capability of tracing students behavior and progresses.

Keywords: Assessment, Programming Assignments, Gamification, Testing.

1 Introduction

Systems for the automated assessment of programs are significant educational tools in computer science teaching. Besides checking and evaluating student's bare programming proficiency, they are important also as a means to improve teaching of algorithmic problem solving [1]. The approaches to the (real time) assessment and feedback for solutions to programming assignments are varied, and based on the two pillars of static and dynamic analysis of programs. In sum, about the importance, and effectiveness, of automated assessment, several analyses are available, concluding that the use of the above mentioned kinds of support is positively useful for students and should be fostered ([2], although in a particular form of code execution support; [1,3,4,5]). Moreover, the increasing attention to massive open on-line courses (MOOCs) is a reason for renewed interest in the area of automatic assessment of students' programs [6]. Although the approach presented in this paper can be applied to MOOC, here we are meeting the problem of automated assessment in a more general view, characterized mainly by the use of gamification features. One significant aspect in a program assignment assessment system is in the fact that some degrees of competition is introduced into the learning process. As a matter of fact, several systems for automated assessment of programs are used in the framework of programming contests, and such contests are an active field of research also for the good return on competence that competition can enable among students [7,8].

On the other hand, competition can in turn be a negative spur for students, conducive to diminished engagement, especially when the system is used on a voluntary self-assessment basis by the students. A sustained engagement in solving exercises is needed, and can be made unavailable by boredom, lack of patience, need to get results in the quickest way, and in general lack for motivation. We thought that some of these engagement problems could be solved by injecting gamification in the process. Gamification is the process of modification of a non-game context (the learning environment), by the integration in it of game design elements and game mechanics. Context, quests, competition, leader board, fast feedback, experience points, achievements, levels, badges, are examples of devices used in a gamified approach, to gain engagement, motivation, and ultimately learning [9,10].

In this paper we present a system (2TSW), supporting automated assessment of programming assignments, in a gamified environment. In 2TSW the student can access a list of programming tasks, propose a solution for some of them, and have it assessed in real time. The assessment is based on unit testing, with tests devised by the teacher at task-definition time. The output of the assessment shows the tests done, the number of points gained (depending on how many tests were passed), and the medal granted for the solution. Tasks are grouped in categories, a category being a set of tasks ranging over the same topic, such as the use of reference pointer, or of a particular data structure. Depending on the tasks solved in a category, and on the solutions' quality, the student is granted a category badge. Several courses can be defined in 2TSW, each one with a teacher as administrator. The overall performance of the student in the course is witnessed by a Status indicator. The 2TSW user interface allows the student to check on her profile achievements (status, category badges, task medals, experience points), to have a visual estimate of her position in the class (how many are her points with respect to the peers) and also to compare her performance with those of others. After the 2TSW presentation, we show a test designed to verify whether the system is fit for use with students. Namely, we are not showing a full experimentation, on whose sole basis the system effectiveness could be evaluated, yet we demonstrate the use of the system along a simulated experimentation: this is based on a sample of artificial students, modelled by defining their attitude and competence; solutions to tasks are submitted, on behalf of the students; quality of the solutions is made dependent on the associated students' models. The simulated experimentation proceeds in two steps, assuming that from the first to the second step the students' capabilities have increased according to their model. So, the aim of the simulated experimentation is to verify whether the system is able to trace the students behavior and the changes in their models, in view of an experimental use with real students.

2 Related Work

Various kinds of automated support to programming education are met in research since decades; work on the topic is, for instance, described in [11]. The widest area of investigation seems to be related to introductory programming courses, where students learn to write programs, according to a programming language syntax and semantics, and to solve problems [6,12].

In program assessment, errors may be uncovered basically by means of two types of program analysis. The first type is Static Analysis, that produces feedback without program execution, based on the program's syntax and static semantics. Approaches of this type can be based on compiler error detection and explanation [12,13], structured similarity between marked and unmarked programs [14], and also nonstructural analysis, with plagiarism detection and keyword search [15]. The second type of analysis works on the dynamic semantics, and possibly the logic, of the program, pointing out errors by means of testing. This means that the program is run over specific sets of input data, devised to unveil problems, with the output compared to the expected one. Competitive learning tools, used to manage programming contests [16] are based on this kind of analysis. Notably [17] combine the two approaches.

[3], describe the BOSS online submission and assessment system. BOSS is a composite system able to receive programming solutions by students and apply to them a collection of predefined tests, in order to assess them. Besides, or flanking, assessment are subsystems dedicated to maintain privacy of the solutions, frame programs in a safe execution environment (sandbox) and check about plagiarism issues. In [1] the system Kattis is described. It is deemed to propose students with programming exercises that can represent a means for both programming practice and access to theoretical aspects, besides allowing for assessment and grading. Kattis is also used to support programming competitions (such as the ACM-ICPC finals).

Approaches based on test driven development (TDD) are also studied, where students are to devise tests to check the correctness of their own programs. [4,18] show that TDD had a positive effect on the ability of students to test their own programs, basing on the use of the system Web-CAT, in the framework of an introductory programming course. An interesting observation stemming from [18] is in that any approach based on automatic testing of programs assigns significant responsibilities to the course staff authoring the programming assignments. The hardship of having to produce tasks "clearly defined, especially with regard to the details of input and output", to devise sound and complete tests, and to "construct a reference solution that has been thoroughly tested", was positively faced in our work with 2TSW too. Another approach dealing with student-provided tests is in [5]. There the student's program is checked basing on her own provided tests, besides the reference tests and solution provided by the teacher.

3 The 2TSW system

2TSW is a web application allowing to define "Course Areas". In a Course Area (CA) students can enroll and have a set of Programming Tasks (PTs) available. A teacher is given responsibility for the CA, where she adds PTs and monitor the students participation. In particular, an enrolled student can access the list of PTs of the course (Fig.1) and submit a solution. Submitted solutions are tested, upon submission, by using unit testing, and the feedback is shown to the student (Fig. 2). The available tasks are actually parted in Categories, whereas a category collects programming exercises on a common Topic. Moreover, each task is assigned a set of Experience Points, depending on its difficulty (the amount of Exp. Points is decided by the teacher, when she adds the task in the system). When a student submits a solution to that task, if the solution passes all the tests it is considered perfect, and the whole lot of Experience Points is granted. Lesser performances let the student gain less points. On the basis of the points gained after a solution, a corresponding task-related medal is granted. A solution can be evaluated as deserving a Gold/Silver/Bronze medal, or a Wooden Spoon.

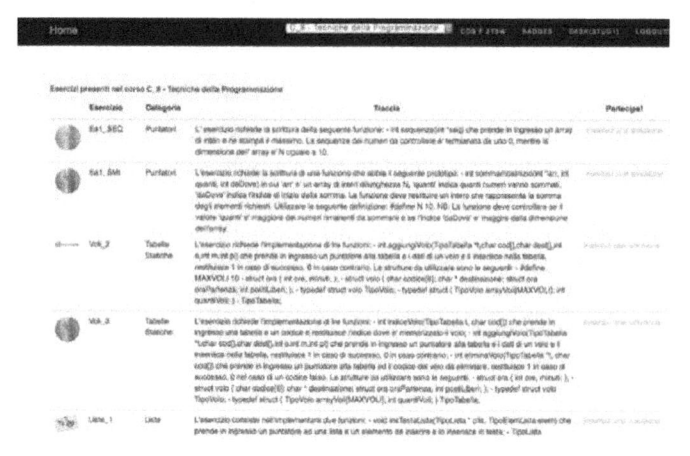

Fig. 1. List of the available programming tasks (description is irrelevant). Three tasks were solved (Gold, Silver, Bronze medals). One task was not successful (Wooden Spoon). One, in this part of the screen, is yet to do.

Basing on the results of the solutions submitted by a student, her "panoply" is maintained (basically that is the student's model). A student's panoply (Fig. 3) shows the general Status of the student, together with the results obtained by her solutions. In particular, for each category a Category Badge is shown, depending on the performance on the tasks in that category.

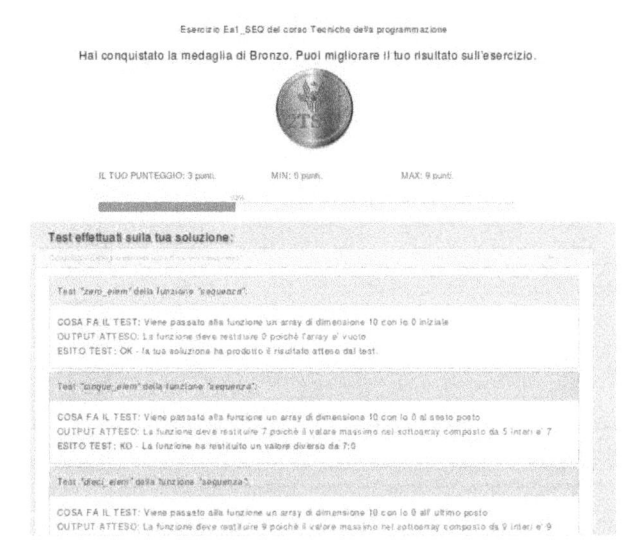

A Gamified Approach to Automated Assessment of Programming Assignments

Fig. 2. The feedback produced by the system about a submitted solution: a medal tells the evaluation (Bronze is less than Silver, which is less than Gold. The Wooden Spoon is the least evaluation). For each test performed on the code, then, the result is shown. The test ration is described, so to allow the student to see through it.

A Category Badge is labelled as Amateur, Beginner, Expert, Champion, or Legend, depending on the ratio between the points gained and those available in the category.

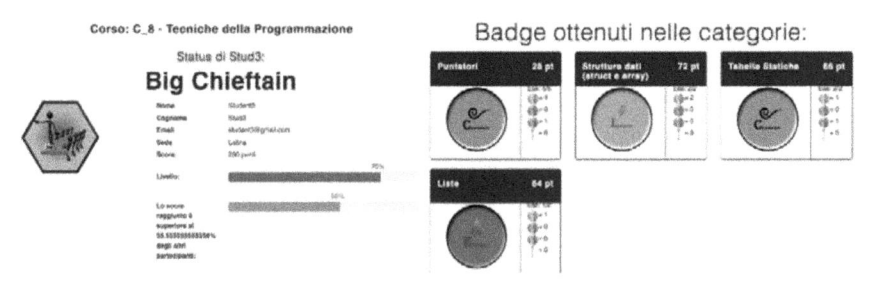

Fig. 3. A student's panoply (grouped to let it fit into this page): the status is shown, together with information about the performance in the categories of tasks. For each category the level (badge), and the medals are shown. A medal, or spoon, is granted for each undertaken task.

In a Category box, after the Category Badge, a summary of the medals gained on the tasks of that category is shown. A student can submit further solutions for the same task, supposedly with the intent of doing better. In these case the last solution is the one considered for the composition of the student's panoply. The Status of a student is computed basing on the overall amount of her Experience Points. The Leader Board (Fig.4) allows the teacher to see through the students' performance, and the students to evaluate and compare their performances. The interface for teacher and student is the same, just the teacher's one can access more data.

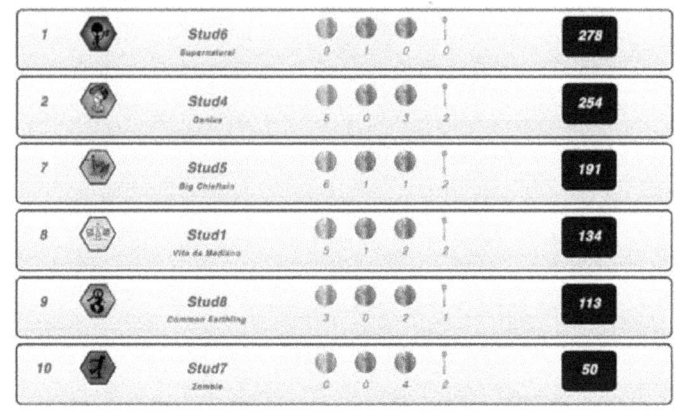

Fig. 4. Fragments of the Leader Board. The Status badges are, in order of programming prowess, Zombie, Common Earthling, Vita_da_mediano (which is a citation from a song, non-translatable; it just means the dull work of a Middlefield player in football), Big Chieftain, Genius, Supernatural, Deity (no Deity in our simulated experiment).

Through the panoply, depending on the privileges, the student and the teacher can access various levels of details about students. Whereas a student can access only basic information about another student, she can access a detailed presentation of each of her solutions (Fig. 5).

Fig. 5. Detailed, visual/textual, presentation of the performance in a task: quality of the solution is shown by the medal and by the Exp. Points gained. The category and the ratio of points gained, against the overall points defined for the task, are also shown.

Moreover, a student can access her "trend", showing the curve of her performance: the performances can be shown in relation to either a single task (by the level of the various solutions proposed for that task), or a category of tasks (showing the curve of evolution of the category badges granted to the student), or the overall status level (which is the case shown in Fig. 6)

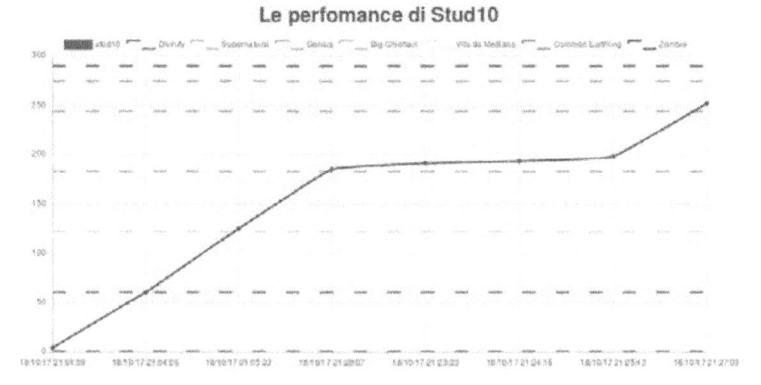

Fig. 6. Trend of the Status level for a student. It shows the evolution of the Status during the work of the student into the system. (in this case from Zombie, to Genius).

4 Putting on trial the system, by a simulated experiment

We intend to pursue an experimentation with students of the first year of a course of Computer Science Foundations, in the Computer Engineering undergraduate study program. At the beginning of the semester it is no time for an effective experimentation, so we decided to perform a preliminary investigation about the system responsiveness to the task. Such investigation is conducted under the form of a simulation of experimentation, in which 10 sim-students are involved. For such purpose we provided a course, with 11 programming tasks, over 4 categories (reference pointer, array/struct, table data structure, list data structure).

We defined the simulated student (s-s) by modelling her *attitude* and *competence*. The *attitude* labels a s-s as either a "Challenger" or a "Minimalist". A Challenger wants to try, and retry the solution of as many tasks as possible, with the aim to advance her qualification as much as possible. Challengers are supposed to aim at the best possible status, and collect the most valuable medals. On the contrary, a Minimalist is supposed to do just what is needed to reach a reasonably good advancement (let's assume that something higher than Zombie would be enough), and probably no task would be attempted more than once, if just it was solved sufficiently. As of the *competence*, it is pointed out by a label (low, average, good, high). During the simulation, the behavior of the students is simulated, letting them undertake programming tasks, and submit solutions, overall according to their individual typology. The simulation flows along two phases: during the first phase each student is let behave according to her initial typology: each student selects a number of tasks, and solves them, according to her typology (see below what behavior we associate to a typology). Depending on the typology the student might also provide more solutions for the same task (only the last one valid for the evaluation), in an effort of make it better.

At the end of the first phase an effect of the activity is hypothesized, i.e. we assume that it is true that the activity supported by the system has positive effects on the students' proficiency. So we change the typology of the s-s, making it, in general, slightly better. During the second phase, the "slightly better" typologies are used, to guide the results of the further s-s' work (further tasks are undertaken). The sample we defined for the simulation, and the development of phase 1, are given in Tab.1.

Table 1. Phase 1: C/M stand for Challenger/Minimalist. Several tasks are undertaken by the sim-students. At the end of the phase a status is achieved; a new typology is assigned, assuming that the activity was beneficial for the s-s. (L/A/G/H = Low, Average, Good, High)

Student	Init. typology	achieved status	new typology
stud1	<C, L>	Common Earthl.	<C, A> (20%-40%)
stud2	<C, A>	vita_da_mediano	<C, A> (40%-60%)
stud3	<C, G>	Big Chieftain	<C, H>
stud4	<C, H>	Genius	<C, H>
stud5	<C, A>	vita_da_mediano	<C, A> (40%-60%)
stud6	<C, G>	Genius	<C, H>
stud7	<M, L>	zombie	<M, L>
stud8	<M, A>	Common Earthl.	<M, A> (20%-40%)
stud9	<M, G>	vita_da_mediano	<M, H>
stud10	<M, H>	Big Chieftain	<M, H>

During the first phase the s-s meets a number of assignments from different categories; a Challenger would try 5-6 tasks, possibly repeating some of them; a Minimalist would try 3-4 tasks, once each. We took care of letting each s-s submit solutions that are coherent with her typology's competence: summing up the overall performance, a high competence s-s would propose solutions getting a number of experience points between 80% and 100% of those defined for the tasks. On the contrary a low competence s-s would gain 0% to 20% of those points. Likewise, an average competence s-s would gain between 20% and 60%: here we defined two sub-levels, equi-distributed (see below, and Tab.3). An s-s with good competence would then gain between 60% and 80% of the available points. For each s-s we submit the devised solutions, while the system does its job and maintain the related Status/category badges, task medals, and experience points for each s-s. The second phase is conducted along the same lines as above, just the *new typologies* are used. In particular, if an s-s's typology shows an "average" competence level, we assume that, solving tasks, 20%-60% of the available points could be gained. We decided to define two different sub-levels in this degree of competence, one where 20%-40% of the points would be gained, and the other in the 40%-60% bracket. During the first phase an "avg" s-s is by default in the first bracket.

During phase 2, again, a Challenger would submit more solutions than a Minimalist (we postulated that attitude would not change in a short term): Tab. 2 shows the tasks met by the s-s in the phases. The final results, coming after the second phase, are shown in Tab. 3. An analysis of the table allows to conclude that the system is able to trace the behavior of the students, as the flow of change in the status is in agreement with the typologies we assigned to the sample students.

Table 2. Phase 1 and 2: number of tasks undertaken by the s-s.

student	phase1 tasks	repeated	phase2 tasks	repeated
Stud1, 2	5	3	5	3
stud3	5	2	5	2
stud4	5	1	5	1
Stud5, 6	5	2	5	2
stud7,8,9	3	0	3	0
stud10	4	0	3	0

Table 3. Results post phase 2. Initial / new typologies are shown. Category badges = A, B, E, C, L (Amateur, Beginner, Expert, Champion, Legend). "Status" and "final status" show how the s-s status changed after phase 2: status names are given as numbers, to allow appreciate the change, so 1,2,3,4,5, 6, resp. stand for Zombie, Common Earthling, Vita da mediano, Big Chieftain, Genius, Supernatural. Notice that different tasks grant different amount of Exp. Points: this explains differences between students with similar cat.badges / number of exercises. Finally Comp. chg / Status chg say how many steps "competence in the s-s typology" / Status raised.

student	s1	s2	s3	s4	s5	s6	s7	s8	s9	s10
typology	C,L	C,A(-)	C,G	C,H	C,A(-)	C,G	M,L	M,A	M,G	M,H
new typ.	C,A(-)	C,A(+)	C,H	C,H	C,G	C,H	M,L	M,A (-)	M,H	M,H
cat1 badge	E	E	C	B	E	E	B	A	--	E
cat2 badge	E	E	L	E	E	E	A	A	E	E
cat3 badge	B	L	C	C	E	L	B	L	L	E
cat4 badge	B	E	C	L	L	L	--	B	L	L
G medals	3	6	8	5	7	9	0	3	5	7
S medals	1	0	0	0	1	0	0	0	0	0
B medals	3	3	2	3	1	0	4	2	1	0
wooden	3	1	0	2	1	1	2	1	0	0
status	2	3	4	5	3	5	1	2	3	4
final status	3	4	5	5	5	6	1	2	5	5
Exp. points	123	206	257	254	251	278	50	113	247	252
Comp. chg	1	1	1	0	2	1	0	0	1	0
Status chg	1	1	1	0	2	1	0	0	2	1
n. tasks	10	10	10	10	10	10	6	6	6	7

In particular, we considered how much the Status changed from phase 1 to phase 2, and how this is corresponding to the changes in typology we stated between the phases (see Tab.3): in general, an advancement in competence between phases (for instance from Good to High) corresponds to a status jump after phase 2 (such as from Big Chieftain to Genius). There are two cases in which this doesn't add up perfectly, showing a greater increase in Status than in Competence: 1) stud9 raises from Good to High competence, and from Vita da Mediano (3) till Genius (5); 2) stud10 doesn't change typology, and gains status from Big Chieftain (4) to Genius. We do think that both exceptions can be explained, as in these cases Competence reached level High, i.e. could then not grow further. In this regard, the difference between the number of labels for competence and status seemed not decisive, in the limited framework of this simulation.

5 Conclusions

We have presented 2TSW, a web based system supporting automated assessment of programming assignments, in a gamified environment, based on devices, such as leader board, badges, comparison (possibly anonymized) with peers, and rendered by means of a highly responsive and dynamic interaction environment. As a means to validate the current 2TSW implementation, we proposed a simulated experimentation, based on the behavior of a sample of artificial students, modelled by attitude and competence. The simulation allowed to conclude that the system is able to trace the students behavior and the changes in their models, and so it would be already fit to support a true experimentation with real students.

References

[1] Enstrom, E., Kreitz, G., Niemela, F., Soderman, P., Kann, V.: Five Years with Kattis – Using an Automated Assessment System in Teaching. In Proc. FIE Conference, IEEE (2011).
[2] Brusilovsky, P., Sosnovsky, S.: Individualized exercises for self-assessment of programming knowledge: An evaluation of QuizPACK. J. Ed. Resources in Computing 5(3) (2005)
[3] Joy, M., Griffiths, N., Boyatt, R.: The BOSS online submission and assessment system. ACM J. Educational Resources in Computing 5(3) (2005)
[4] Edwards, S.H., Perez-Quinones, M.A.: Web-CAT: automatically grading programming assignments. In Proc. ITiCSE, pp. 328–328, ACM (2008)
[5] de Souza, D.M., Maldonado, J.C., Barbosa, E.F.: ProgTest: An environment for the submission and evaluation of programming assignments. In Proc. SEET, IEEE (2011).
[6] Pieterse, V.: Automated Assessment of Programming Assignments. In Proc. CSERC (2013).
[7] Dagienė, V.: Sustaining informatics education by contests. In: Teaching Fundamentals Concepts of Informatics. Springer, 1–12 (2010)
[8] Combéfis, S., Wautelet, J.: Programming trainings and informatics teaching through online contests. Olympiads in Informatics, p. 21 (2014)
[9] Deterding, S., Dixon, D., Khaled, R., Nacke, L.: From Game Design Elements to Gamefulness: Defining "Gamification", In Proc. MindTrek'11, ACM (2011)
[10] Kapp, K. M.: The gamification of learning and instruction: Game-based methods and strategies for training and education. John Wiley & Sons (2012)
[11] Hollingsworth, J.: Automatic graders for programming classes. Comm. ACM 3, 10 (1960).
[12] Hristova, M., Misra, A., Rutter, M., Mercuri, R.: Identifying and Correcting Java Programming Errors for Introductory Computer Science Students. SIGCSE '03 (2003).
[13] Watson, C., Li, F., Godwin, J.: Bluefix: Using crowd-sourced feedback to support programming students in error diagnosis and repair. ICWL2012, LNCS 755, Springer (2012).
[14] Naudé, K., Greyling, J., Vogts, D.: Marking student programs using graph similarity. Comp. and Ed., 54, pp. 545–561, (2010).
[15] Khirulnizam, A., Md, J.: A review on the static analysis approach in the automated programming assessment systems. Nat. Conf. on Soft. Eng. and Comp. Systems (2007).
[16] Leal, J., Silva, F.: Mooshak: a web-based multi-site programming contest system. Software: Practice and Experience, 33, pp. 567–581 (2003).
[17] Wang, T., Su, P., Ma, X., Wang, Y., Wang, K.: Ability-training-oriented automated assessment in introductory programming course. Comp. and Ed., 56, pp. 220–226, (2011).
[18] Edwards, S.H.: Improving student performance by evaluating how well students test their own programs. J. Educational Resources in Computing 3(3) (2003).

A Smart Learning Environment for Environmental Education

Ilkka Jormanainen[1*], Tapani Toivonen[1], and Ville Nivalainen[2]

[1] University of Eastern Finland, School of Computing, Finland
[2] City of Joensuu, Finland
ville.nivalainen@jns.fi

Abstract. Environmental education is nowadays an important part of school curricula everywhere. We have built a novel learning environment based on Internet of Things technologies, such as sensor networks and cloud storages. Initial tests of the learning environment indicate that local sensor data is an effective way to adapt multidisciplinary projects and scaffold learning for different age groups in a single learning environment.

Keywords: Environmental education, internet of things, sensor networks, contextualized learning.

1 Introduction

Climate change is one of the global major challenges that prevails discussion in many levels of the society. Governments are setting global goals and assessing trends for sustainable development in order to reduce impact of the climate change and global warming. Equally, countless companies, NGOs, school organizations, and individuals are facilitating campaigns, activities, and personal interventions to minimize impact of their actions. City of Joensuu in eastern Finland aims to achieve carbon neutrality by 2025. This means that by this year, net carbon footprint (CFP[1]) of the city should be neutral, in other words the city produces carbon dioxide emissions just as much as it can sequester or offset. An important part of this aim is school education, and how climate change is integrated into school curricula.

To improve environmental education and proceed with the CFP reducing cause, an experimental learning environment *HiljaNet* for observing CFP and energy

---

[1] Carbon footprint (CFP) is one of the globally accepted measure to assess environmental impact of a product, a process, or an activity. CFP measures amount of carbon dioxide and other greenhouse gas emissions during the lifecycle of the product, or how much greenhouse gases are emitted during an event or by an individual.

consumption in local Karhunmäki primary school was developed. HiljaNet learning environment is based on distributed sensor network that integrates in building automation and measures for example electricity and water consumption in several locations, room temperature and carbon dioxide concentration, current weather conditions, and electricity production from the building's solar panel system. All these measurements can be observed individually, compared with each other, and the system uses them to calculate automatically the carbon footprint of the school environment. Teachers of the school can use HiljaNet as a platform to build contextualized exercises and projects that are bound to the school's curriculum and multidisciplinary projects. In this paper, we present the initial implementation of HiljaNet with discussion about its implications to environmental education and projects in the school.

2   Background and related work

IT driven learning environments for environmental education exist in many forms. For example, Weeks et al. [3] present a mobile application to develop students' knowledge about energy sustainability. The application presented in the paper uses collaborative learning and expert knowledge in learning. However, in contrast to HiljaNet, the application presented in Weeks et al. [3] does not ground learning to locally produced data. As another example, Peters and Butler Songer [2] present an application of Interactive Map activity for climate change education. The research shows that students had difficulties on making meaningful connections between map overlays and data they represented, hence connection to curricular content remained vague. Bodzin, on the other hand, argues [1] that integrating IT solutions with locally available data and local context motivates students in environmental education. Following this argument, our hypothesis is that local HiljaNet data sources facilitate learning better than observing more general data fetched from remote sources or databases. Making connections to surrounding environment and possibility to map sensor data to currently experienced conditions may help students to scaffold learning content in a novel way. Two of the overarching goals of the new Finnish curricula are ICT skills and awareness for sustainable way of living. In practice, this means a requirement to integrate ICT efficiently to all subjects, including advanced skills such as computational thinking, programming, and information retrieval and visualization. Environmental education should be reflected in the same way in all subjects. These were important factors that motivated development of HiljaNet.

3   HiljaNet learning environment

HiljaNet is built on top of a commercial Internet of Things platform. The system is built by Sensire Ltd[2]., a company focusing on providing IoT services to monitor distribution and delivery chains in pharmaceutical and food industry. The company was selected to implement HiljaNet because their sensor technology was readily deployed in the school building as part of building automation and catering services. Additional sensors and services such as a local weather station, were installed to enhance functionality of HiljaNet. The sensor network comprises about 40 different measuring points for collecting data about energy and electricity consumption. Furthermore, the system measures how much electricity the solar panels installed in the roof of the school building produce. All sensors record a data point every 15 minutes and measured data is saved to a cloud storage.

HiljaNet is a browser-based application and it consumes sensor data providing high

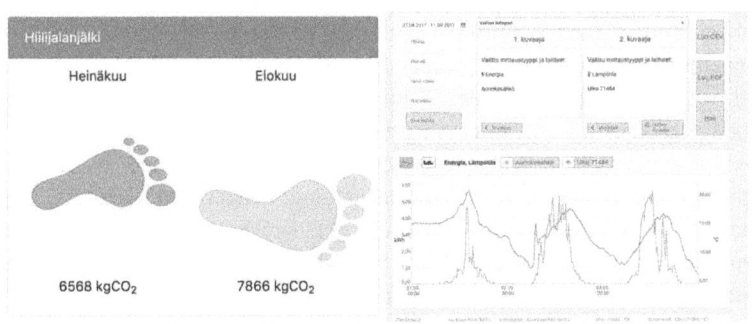

Fig. 1. HiljaNet provides visualizations on different abstraction levels.

level visualizations (Figure 1, left) and more detailed views for sensor information (Figure 1, right). Students can search and explore information and combine sensors into graph visualizations (c.f. Figure 1) to learn about different phenomena, for example how much solar energy is needed to compensate carbon footprint that was caused by consumption of hot water in the school building shower facilities. In this way, with the HiljaNet students can actively build their understanding how their own actions can reduce school environment's carbon footprint. Teachers' active participation helped to define pedagogically meaningful tasks and projects for different student groups. In all tasks, the starting point is that the students can observe, explore, and retrieve information about different sensors and environmental conditions from the HiljaNet. Examples of these tasks are as follows.

- **Grades 1-2 (7-8 years old students):** What happens to energy consumption of the school building when weather gets colder outside? Why this happens?
- **Grades 3-6 (9-12 years):** How much money will be saved when part of electricity needed in the school is produced with the solar panels? How weather in different seasons affect to this?

---

[2] https://www.sensire.com/

- **Grades 7-9 (13-15 years):** Trees can absorb CO2 from air. How many trees of specified types the students should plant at the end of school year to compensate the carbon footprint caused by factors that root from their own choices?

4 Conclusion

We have presented HiljaNet, a novel learning platform for environmental education. The system is based on IoT technologies and embodies a sensor network installed in the school building. By having a contextual and real-time data available, students can work in multidisciplinary projects exploring different phenomena and learn environmental awareness on the same time. For teachers, HiljaNet provides an efficient way to scaffold teaching with pedagogically meaningful content for different age groups in a single learning environment that supports and encourages students for collaborative and exploratory learning. Our future work includes developing visualizations further and leveraging educational data mining and machine learning methods to provide more personalized and contextual learning experience, and to develop HiljaNet towards a full-scale smart learning environment. Also, learning environments' effect in learning need to be studied further.

References

[1] Bodzin, A. M.: Integrating Instructional Technologies in a Local Watershed Investigation With Urban Elementary Learners. In: The Journal of Environmental Education, 39(2), pp. 47-58. Routledge (2008).
[2] Peters, V., Butler Songer, N.: Evaluating the usability of an interactive map activity for climate change education. In: Proceedings of the 10th International Conference on Interaction Design and Children (IDC '11), pp. 197-200. ACM, New York, NY, USA (2011).
[3] Weeks, C., Delalonde, C., Preist, C.: The use of Digital Technology to Evaluate School Pupils' Grasp of Energy Sustainability. In: Proceedings of the 2016 CHI Conference Extended Abstracts on Human Factors in Computing Systems (CHI EA '16), pp. 1308-1314, ACM, New York, NY, USA (2016).

An interdisciplinary Framework for Designing Smart Learning Environments

Sirkka Freigang[1], Lars Schlenker[2] and Thomas Köhler[2]

[1] Bosch Software Innovations, Berlin, Germany
sirkka.freigang@bosch-si.com
[2] Dresden University of Technology, Institute for Vocational Education, Dresden, Germany
{lars.schlenker, thomas.koehler}@tu-dresden.de

Abstract. The paper deals with the role of Smart Learning Environments (SLEs) in the field of corporate education and the need for their interdisciplinary design in the face of existing problems with the introduction of Technology-Enhanced Learning (TEL). For a human-centered design of SLEs new concepts and models have to be developed in order to meet the complex requirements of the 21st century. Authors describe an interdisciplinary research approach for designing SLEs and discuss a holistic, socio-technical framework combining interdisciplinary criteria for an educationally profound development of SLEs while the presentation of the subject, based on current findings from a research project at TU Dresden, a leading German University of Technology. With the question of how an interdisciplinary approach of education, computer science and architecture contributes to SLE-design, the study empirically applies data collected in 2016.

Keywords: Smart Learning Environments; Further Education; Interdisciplinarity

1 TEL in Vocational Education and Training

The successful and sustainable use of technologies in corporate training requires far more preparatory work of conceptual and didactic nature than the sole provision of technology [1]. Modern digital education formats must be aligned to a learners' individual needs, easy to use and utilizable via various devices. In the context of a constructivist theory of teaching and learning, vocational-education approaches argue that situated, self-regulated, explorative and collaborative learning methods are particularly suited, to strengthen learning processes in general. Yet in the case of lifelong learning, which is getting more and more important in relation to digitization, individuals need fluent forms of learning, which calls for smart learning approaches. Eventually, one may learn from the past, i.e. take those TEL approaches into account that may overcome isolated achievements - like smart learning. Previously TEL has not succeeded in revolutionizing education, most likely because TEL initiatives often take a centralized technology-push approach.

Recently, the Smart Learning Environment (SLE) concept has emerged and opens new doors for more efficient learning by overcoming many of the limitations of traditional TEL models. However, to be successful, one needs a systematic design process of SLEs, considering influential domains overarchingly. Identifying relevant areas and success factors supports the design process in a structured way. Within such a framework, educationalist are able to create meaningful SLEs, based on conceptual, human-centered and didactic principles. In the following, authors present the role of SLEs and the design requirements, considering the above-mentioned circumstances for didactically profound models of vocational education.

2 The design of SLEs as an interdisciplinary challenge

There is no standardized definition of SLEs. According to [2], SLEs are physical environments enriched with digital and context-sensitive components to enable faster and better learning. This definition shows the particular importance of the learning space, and although [2] defines SLEs as physical environments the architecture of spaces and effects of spatial design on learning processes do not play a role in the current SLE research. Accordingly, educational sciences as well as information technology and spatial sociological aspects shall be taken into account when designing innovative learning rooms like SLEs – which is not new for designing learning technologies [3].

2.1 Research approach, methodology and first results

On that basis, an interdisciplinary approach was chosen within the scope of an ongoing research project on the role of the "Internet of Things" (IoT) in intelligent learning spaces. Focusing on the interweaving of the disciplines mentioned above one of the research questions aimed at the development of a didactically sound concept for the design of SLEs by using the IoT concept for learning purposes. Against the background of a design-based research approach, a triangulative study of exploratory character was carried out. Based on interdisciplinary literature reviews, a first model could worked out, which identified core categories in the SLE design process and defined success factors. According to Spector's "preliminary framework for smart learning environments" [1], philosophical, psychological and technological approaches were condensed in a first socio-technical model. The model consists of two dimensions, each with three categories[1], interacting with each other. This model served as a search grid for the empirical study and was a partial

---

[1] Cf. further explanations to the six categories online on the Bosch Blog: "IoT in education by designing smart learning environments"

An interdisciplinary Framework for Designing Smart Learning Environments 19

presumption derived from the literature reviews. The subsequent multi-level data collection consisted of a focus group workshop (summer 2016) in combination with a quantitative questionnaire (sub study 1) and nine expert interviews (winter 2016), which were supplemented with questionnaires (sub study 2). In order to derive precise recommendations for action, the models extracted SLE attributes (46 items in total) were summarized in an evaluation sheet of sub study 2, which in addition to a qualitative expert survey was a quantitative element of the triangulative study. The characteristics were assessed on a scale from 1 = very important to 5 = unimportant with regard to their meaning for the design of SLEs. The aim of sub study 2 was to find out whether the significance of the characteristics of the six interdisciplinary areas can also be "confirmed" empirically. Therefore a hypothetical model was presented to experts right after an interview by brief explanation. Afterwards, a systematic evaluation carried out within the sub study 2 used quantitative questionnaires and based on that expert assessment four most important items per category were found as shown in figure 1.

Fig.1. SLE framework with most important items per category (Source: authors' graphic)

The quantitative data analysis (Table 1) finds items correlated very strongly within the respective category and subsequently grouped into one scale per category2. The descriptive statistics shows the following mean values per category:

Table 1. Mean values of the six SLE categories

Category	N	Minimum	Maximum	Mean value	Standard-deviations
Learner Needs	9	1	3,22	2,0494	0,65

---

[2] For scale creation, a mean value has been calculated for each item. Despite the small sample size, the scales show an acceptable to good reliability ($\alpha=.70$ to $\alpha=.90$).

Learning & Working methods	9	1	3,83	2,1481	0,82
Learning & organizational culture	9	1	2,33	1,8148	0,46
Technology	9	1	3,75	2,3981	0,75
Digital & physical Equipment	9	1	2,86	2,0794	0,58
Workplace Architecture	9	1	3,33	1,9815	0,68

As first result experts concluded the model being suitable for developing didactically meaningful SLEs. Due to the small sample (n = 9) the quantitative evaluation is not representative, but is to be interpreted on a case-basis. This first model was validated within a focus group workshop and an interview study qualitatively. A modified re-design of the framework based on the completed empirical data analysis will be presented at the International Conference on SLE in March 2018.

3 Conclusion

Identified SLE-characteristics are important across all domains and should therefore be addressed when designing SLEs. Furthermore, findings support the assumption of an interdisciplinary approach being useful for the design of SLEs. Complex hybrid constructs such as SLEs can only be understood and made meaningful by bundling interdisciplinary knowledge. With that TEL becomes an even stronger cross-disciplinary endeavour, calling for a new awareness of both the producers of educational contents as well as the learners [4], [5]. For further SLE-research adjacent disciplines must be reflected and integrated into the research framework to investigate causal relationships. An appropriate design-oriented education research with close feedback processes to spatial, information- and media-technological design would open up new perspectives with regard to the development of technology-enhanced teaching and learning environments.

4 References

[1] Spector, J. M. (2014). Conceptualizing the emerging field of smart learning environments. Smart Learning Environments 1, 1–10

[2] Koper, R. (2014). Conditions for effective smart learning environments. Smart Learning Environments 1, 1–17

[3] Reitmaier, M., Köhler, T. & Apollon, D. (2011). Rollen bei der Entwicklung von multimedialen Lernangeboten; In: Köhler, T., & Neumann, J. Wissensgemeinschaften. Digitale Medien – Öffnung und Offenheit in Forschung und Lehre; Münster, Waxmann.

[4] Marquet, P. & Köhler, T. (2017). The empowerment of users: rethinking educational practice online; In: Dobrick, F. M. et al.: Research Ethics in the Digital Age. Ethics for the Social Sciences and Humanities in Times of Mediatization and Digitization; Berlin, Springer.

[5] Stützer, C. M., Carley, K. M., Köhler, T. & Thiem, G. (2011). The communication infrastructure during the learning process in web based collaborative learning systems; Web Science 2013 Proceedings; ACM Copyright.

Application Development on Tablet to Promote a Classroom Research Skills for SSRU' Students

Chaiwat Waree[1,*]

[1] Faculty of Education, Suan Sunandha Rajabhat University, Bangkok, Thailand
Chaiwat.wa@ssru.ac.th

Abstract. The objectives of this research are: to develop and discover efficiency of application on tablet to promote a classroom research skills for SSRU' students to meet with criteria at 80/80 and to study satisfaction level of students by using application on tablet. The target group herein was 125 students who studied in Academic year of 2014 and interested in online registration. Target group was determined by using purposive sampling. Tools used in this research were 40 items of post-test contained in application on tablet, student's satisfaction evaluation form towards application on tablet usage. Data analysis was conducted to find efficiency of application on tablet as defined by criteria at 80.77/ 81.82 and student's satisfaction level towards application on tablet usage of 125 students. The obtained mean was 4.35 and standard deviation was 0.68. The results showed that the efficiency of application on tablet was at 80.77/ 81.82 that was higher than defined criteria at 80/80. In addition, Overall satisfaction of students towards application on tablet usage was in the highest level with the mean of 4.35 and standard deviation at 0.68. The obtained results were able to be used as guidelines for further development of learning activities management of other courses.

Keywords: Application on Tablet • A Classroom Research Skills • Learning •higher education

1 Introduction

Jiraporn Siritawee [1] who said that the project is the way to teach students to learn how to make a small project that the learner would take action in order to improve their knowledge, skills, creating the quality production with the scientific methodology procedures. The main objective is to stimulate the student to observe, question, create hypothesis, self-learning, conclude and understand what they found. Moreover, project-based learning also has the objective to encourage students to improve their self-learning by emphasizing thinking method and learning process from observing, questioning, experiments, analyzing, and self-creating knowledge Teerachai Puranachoti, [2] that the project-based learning is applied by various techniques as follows, group learning, thinking, problem solving, emphasizing in quiz-based learning, and collaborated thinking. Besides, this aims the students to learn one of the topic from their own interests by using scientific procedure and methodology so the students have to perform activities to find the answer by themselves Colly, K.B.,[3]. Besides from the project-based learning, scientific process skills would also use in other learning such as scientific inquiry and problem-based learning: PBL. So the System Thinking is one of the language forms for explanation and creates a deep understanding about relationship between the factors which lead to the changing of system behavior to the right direction. To practice and perform according to this concept, it is necessary to improve the awareness in complexity of problem and relationship of each factors so the System Thinking is counted as the thinking form that conform to the Higher Order Thinking that sees the problem or problem situation and problem complexity that divided into 3 levels. Besides, the result acquired from using System Thinking is the ability of students to see and understand the situation that requires the work or activity to be effectively operated then it is necessary to supervise or control factor, cause, or issues to prevent the unwanted condition to be occurred Montree Yamkasikorn [4].

Such as, the researcher was interested in electronic media and utilizing innovation to convey an application on tablet to promote a classroom research skills for SSRU' students.

2   Objectives

To create an application on tablet to promote a classroom research skills for SSRU' students to gain efficiency at 80/80 and achieve better level of student's satisfaction.

3   Research Process

1. Studied papers and researches in order to synthesize a classroom research skills. Subsequently, the obtained results were classified , arranged systematically and created in the form of application on tablet.
2. The principle of application by ADDIE model contains Analysis , Design , Development , Implementation and Evaluation. Java is used to write applications installed on the Android operating system. PHP language used in the web server to upload files and chat.
3. Submit developed application on tablet to promote a classroom research skills for SSRU' students to experts for inspection and improvement.

4. Tried out improved application on tablet to promote a classroom research skills for SSRU' students with students who were not target group for further improvement and public relations.

5. Students who were target group studied created application on tablet to promote a classroom research skills and took pre and post test. Subsequently, satisfaction of students was evaluated after their usage of application on tablet.

5.1. Tested students with test review of 3 online lessons. The obtained scores were collected as scores of formative evaluation.

5.2. 40 items of achievement test on online lessons were tested with students and the obtained scores were collected as scores of post-test.

5.3. 10 items of satisfaction evaluation form towards online lessons were commented by students.

6. The results were checked and the obtained scores of pre and post test were analyzed by using statistics in order to find efficiency at 80/80.

7. Student's satisfaction after using application on tablet to promote a classroom research skills was analyzed and concluded.

4 Conclusion

1. From try out of application on tablet, it was found that efficiency of process (E1) provided in tests was calculated to be 80.77% and efficiency of results (E2) was calculated to be 81.82 %. These application on tablet to promote a classroom research skills had higher efficiency than 80/80 as defined therefore it could be concluded that these application on tablet had high efficiency as defined by criteria and they were able to be used for classroom instruction efficiently.

2. From the results of student's satisfaction towards learning with application on tablet, it was found that overall student's satisfaction towards instruction using application on tablet was in the highest level, i.e., students had overall satisfaction towards application on tablet in high level with mean of 4.35 and item 10 was gained the highest satisfaction level of students. Average demand of students on creating application on tablet for other subjects was 4.84. For other evaluations, most of them had high level of satisfaction.

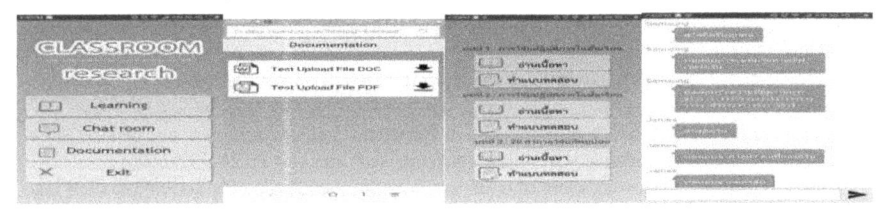

Fig.1. application on tablet to promote a classroom research skills

5 Discussion

- Efficiency of these application on tablet was in high level as expected at 80.77/ 81.82 due to creation and development of such application on tablet. The researcher studied on basic data and analyzed work, contents, students who were target group, and behavioral objectives prior planning on creation and development to meet those behavioral objectives under explanation and suggestions of content expert for inspecting accuracy of contents, language correctness, appropriateness of design, instructional methods, and presentation. Subsequently, the obtained lessons were improved, developed, and tried out with a small student group in order to find further faults for additional improvement and development prior performing field tryout with 40 students. The results showed that efficiency of application on tablet was 80.77/ 81.82 that was satisfying and met with expected hypothesis.
- Student's satisfaction towards application on tablet to promote a classroom research skills was in high level for all items because the research studied on psychology of learning of students before planning creation of application on tablet. Subsequently, the obtained results were planned for creation and development of complete application on tablet that was consistent with work of Chaiwat Waree who studied on Development of online lessons of Suan Sunandha local wisdom for preparing readiness for ASEAN. The results showed that the efficiency of online lessons of Suan Sunandha local wisdom was at 86.00 / 87.50 that was higher than defined criteria at 80/80. In addition, Overall satisfaction of students towards online lessons usage was in the highest level with the mean of 4.46 and standard deviation at 0.68. [5].

Acknowledgements. This research was supported by SSRU and Higher Education Research Promotion (HERP) in Office of the Higher Education Commission. Special thanks you to all experts and students of SSRU who helped and supported this project.

References

[1] Siritawee, J.: Project of creating alternative ways of creating intellectuals. Academic Journal. August, (1999)
[2] Puranachoti, T.: Activities Teaching Science Project. Bangkok: Chulalongkorn University, (1988)
[3] Colly, K. E.: "Understanding ecology content knowledge and acquiring science process skills through project-based science instruction". Science activities. 43(1): 26-33, (2006)
[4] Yamkasikorn, M.: A Development of teaching model for developing the systematic thinking process of undergraduate student. Department of Educational Technology Master Thesis: Srinakharinwirot University, (2003)
[5] Waree, C. :A Development of online lessons of Suansunandha local wisdom for preparing readiness for ASEAN. Bangkok : Rajabhat Suan Sunandha University, (2014)

Constructing a Smart Chinese International Learning Environment Based on Learning Analytics Technology

Juan Xu[1], Yanlan Shi[2], Yongbin Zhou[3]

[1] Director of Smart Learning, Beijing Language and Culture University
xujuan@blcu.edu.cn
[2] Chinese Instructor, Beijing Language and Culture University & Confucius Institute at University of South Carolina   shiyanlan@163.com
[3] Technical Support, Beijing Language and Culture University
zhouyongbinhappy@163.com

Abstract: This essay applies the concept of Smart Learning based on learning analytics technology. The Chinese grammar self-adaptive-adjusting learning system works by constructing a user data set that records the learners' learning behavior and progress, then uses the date to collect on an adaptive mechanism to provide learners with advices, suitable exercises, related questions based on the user model. By making design and implementation of Smart Learning environments, the system can also present a detailed information of the learner's progress in a visual way.

Keywords: Smart Chinese International Learning; Grammar Adaptive Learning System; Complex Sentence Type; Learning Analytics Technology

1. Introduction

Researchers try to build a personalized knowledge awareness map system under Smart Learning Environment. It aims at improving the intelligence level of the existing digital education system and achieving the deep integration of information technology and mainstream education. It promotes the development of information technology and education stakeholders (students, teachers, parents, managers, the public, etc.) The core of Smart Learning is the concept that learning should serve for the better development of the learner's state of mind and abilities [1].

2. Smart Chinese International Learning Based on Learning Analytics Technology

The Smart Chinese learning system is a kind of flexible personalized learning system which is essentially supported by online learning environment. Learning analytics technology has already been viewed as the third wave of enormous education development since the creation of the learning management system [2]. Smart Learning system is able to extract the implied and potential valuable information during the process of "teaching and learning". Learning analytics technology provides smart and flexible suggestions for educator's teaching, student's learning, and overall teaching management [3].

The Chinese adaptive learning system mainly focuses on the complex sentences part of Chinese grammar. A Smart Chinese international learning environment design model is shown in Figure 1. This system contains three main modules: Data source tier, user model and recommendation engine, application display tier. The data source tier includes a grammar knowledge base, including grammar practice test bank. The user model and recommendation engine module include a personalized user model and an adaptive learning recommendation engine. The application display tier includes three parts---the grammar learning, practice and pace of learning. The three modules form a Chinese language syntax adaptive learning system.

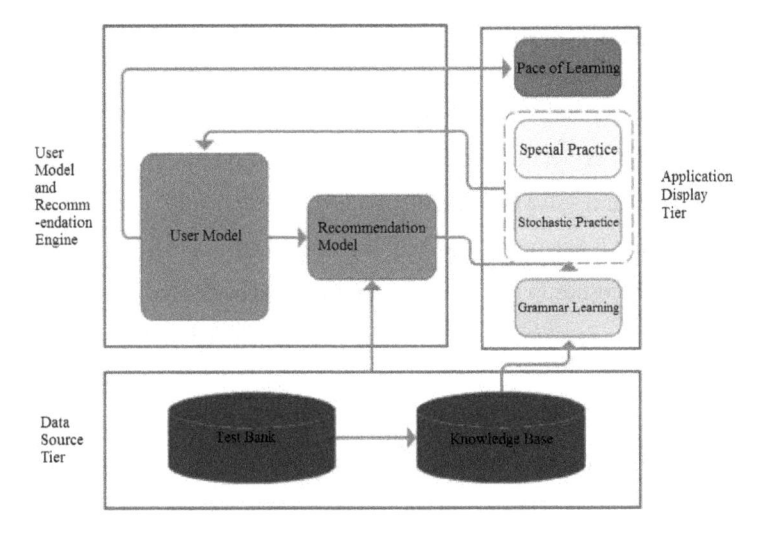

Fig. 1. The model of environment design on Smart Chinese International Learning

3. Data Source Tier

3.1 Knowledge Base of Chinese Grammar

The knowledge Base of Chinese grammar separates grammar contents into 4 levels by difficulty: There are 12 types of Chinese complex sentence forms: Coordinate, Continuous, Selective, Cause-Effect, Transitional, Hypothesis, Purposeful, Progressive, Conditional, Concession, Explanatory, and Contracted Complex Sentence. The database collects 90 kinds of different grammatical features that are contained in the 12 complex sentence formations. The grammar knowledge base uses many resources to enhance its applicability, such as corpus, textbooks, teaching materials. The database contains translation media tools, accurate descriptions, examples, easily mistaken problems, and the difficulty in mastering them.

3.2 Test Bank of Chinese Grammar

This system provides a gradually increasing difficulty on mastering the grammar points for every complex sentence type. We design a lot of questions to evaluate students' grammar level and solve their problems. With the difficulty level rise, the number of distribution of the questions will increase. There are in total 1032 questions of various difficulties in this Chinese grammar test bank, that can provide an accurate account on the mastery of all grammar points included in the database.

4. User Model and Recommendation Engine

There are three user models that contain the user's information-- the learner's basic identification model, the learner's behavior model, and the learner's progress model. The three user models record learner's personal information, analyse learner's activities and efficiency, show learner's mastery on different grammar points. This system automatically evaluates learner's performance, recommends appropriate type of questions and exercises. If a particular grammar point is not fully mastered, this Chinese adaptive learning system will change the progress model, make future approaches to this particular grammar point.

5. Application Display Tier

The application display tier is separated into three different modules-- grammar learning module, grammar practice module, and progress overview module. The user of this tier can enter a selection list of the complex sentence type (Figure 2). Learner's learning is personalized by the system. Different indexes are created for different choices, and the resources collected in the database will be provided accordingly. Every complex sentence tape is noted with detailed explanation, pragmatic examples, pictures and video resources.

Constructing a Smart Chinese International Learning Environment Based ...   29

Fig. 2. Selection of complex sentence types

The grammar practice module can provide specific training for on a particular recommended topic. After the user turns in answers, the system automatically grade the questions and give accurate feedback on the learner's level of mastery in all grammar points based on the difficulty of questions, category of topics, and accuracy of answers (Figure 3). The user can get a detailed and complete look of the learning progress.

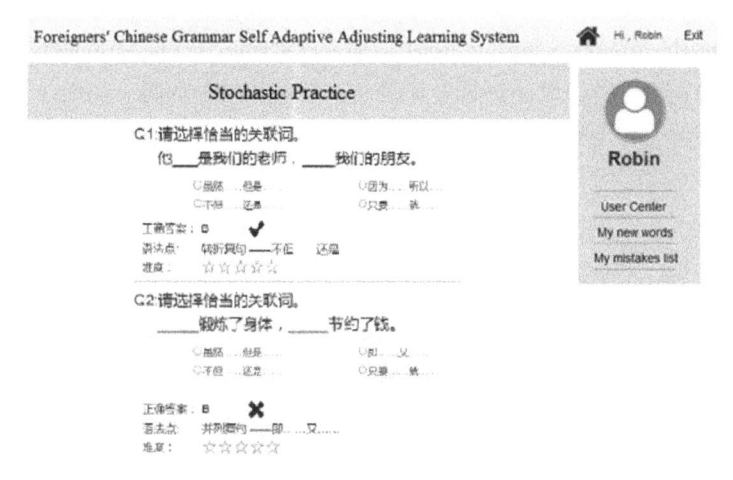

Fig. 3. Examples of answer result feedback

The studying progress review module uses graphs to give the users a clear picture of one's progress, it displays the pace of learning in a graphical way, it is a visualization module. The degree of mastery will be clearly shown as a bar-graph. The progress in a grammar point will be indicated by different depth of color.

6. Summary

Smart Learning is a new method of education built upon developments in information technology. It is a revolutionary change from traditional education methods [4]. This research has completed the self-adapting system concerning complex sentence types, it will continue to construct other self-adapting systems for International Chinese language learning. Smart Learning environment can help students to assess their academic progress, predict their future performance, discover their potential problems and get effective suggestions. Therefore, every student can get high quality and personalized educational services.

Acknowledgements

This paper is supported by 2015 Humanities and Social Sciences Fund Project of Chinese Ministry of Education (NO. 15YJAZH089). The project title is Empirical research of learning analytics in flipped classroom of teaching Chinese to speakers of other languages.

References

[1] Xianmin Yang.: The Connotation and Characteristics of Smart Education in Information Age (in Chinese). China Educational Technology. 324, 29–34 (2014)

[2] Zhiting Zhu, Demei Shen.: Learning Analytics: the Scientific Power in Smart Education (in Chinese). e-Education Research. 241, 5–11 (2013)

[3] Kekang He.: The New Development of "Learning Analytics Technology" in China (in Chinese). e-Education Research. 279, 7–13 (2016)

[4] Ronghuai Huang.: Three Realms of Smart Education: Smart Learning Environment, ICT Teaching Model and Modern Educational System (in Chinese). Modern Distance Education Research. 132, 3–11 (2014)

Effects of Reciprocal Feedback on EFL Learners' Communication Strategy Use and Oral Communicative Performance

Sie Wai Chew[1], Wei-Chieh Fang[2], Chia-Ning Hsu[1], and Nian-Shing Chen[2*]

[1] Department of Information Management, National Sun Yat-sen University, Taiwan
chewsw@mis.nsysu.edu.tw, preetyrabbit@gmail.com,
nschen@mis.nsysu.edu.tw
[2] Washington University in St Louis, MO, USA
wfjohnny@gmail.com

Abstract. While most studies focus on individual training of oral communication strategy use and oral communication performance in English as a Foreign Language (EFL), this study examines the effect of peer review from a socio-constructivist perspective. A mobile application, named Speaking Yo, was developed to facilitate learners to engage in discussion tasks, replay their conversation as well as carry out peer review. A quasi-experiment was conducted in a vocational university in Taiwan for four weeks. Forty EFL participants were assigned to an experimental group ($n = 20$), who received peer feedback, and a control group ($n = 20$), who received no peer feedback. The results showed that the use of peer feedback enhanced students' oral communication performance. However, the use of communication strategies was not improved. The findings suggest that with the support of Speaking Yo, students were able to monitor their oral production and provides/receives corrective feedback on their overall communication performance. However, the feedback provided by the peers was not concrete enough to address the use of communication strategies. The possible explanations and future directions are also discussed in this study.

Keywords: Mobile Learning · Sociocultural Learning · Peer Feedback · Oral Communication Strategy · Oral Communication Performance

1 Introduction

The ability for EFL (English as Foreign Language) learners to perform oral communication requires not only linguistic knowledge but also strategic knowledge. Communication strategies in particular have been found to play a crucial role in communication performance. EFL learners can use communication strategies to compensate for their insufficient linguistic competence when there is a conversation breakdown [1, 10]. Also, developing learners' negotiating strategies for communication can enhance learners' oral proficiency. Through negotiating, learners would modify the linguistic input to make it more intellectual, or comprehensible, for the interlocutors and seek for linguistic knowledge they lack [4, 10]. Studies have found that raising learners' awareness of the communicative strategies improves their use of communication strategy and oral communication ability [8, 10].

While the majority of these studies took a cognitive constructivism approach, which focuses on how individuals develop the communication strategies through instruction and tasks, little research has addressed such development from a sociocultural perspective. Peer feedback, for example, is lacking in the EFL speaking literature [9]. One possible explanation is that oral production, unlike writing, is fleeting and hard to keep track of for learners to work on. To address this problem, researchers have long proposed that audio/video analysis of discourse should be integrated into courses to raise learners' meta-cognitive awareness [2]. Thus, combining mobile learning which provides collaborative and instant interaction as well as recording tool, this study developed a mobile application, called Speaking Yo, to explore the effects of peer feedback on EFL learners' strategic use and oral communicative performance.

2 Literature Review

Communication strategies, hereafter referred to as CS, are the interactional strategies that interlocutors use to cope with communication breakdowns (Nakatani, 2005). Several experimental studies on EFL training CS have emphasized how conscious-raising can facilitate learners' communication strategies and communication ability [7]. For example, Rabab'ah compared the effects of direct CS training with that of a communicative class which did not receive any CS instruction [10]. Learners went through four phases of instructional sequence: (1) consciousness-raising, (2) use of pre-fabricated patterns, (3) engagement in communicative activities, and (4) recording and evaluation. Seven CS, i.e., appeal for help, confirmation checks, and clarification request, were adapted in the study. Generally, the emphasis was on the use of prefabricated expressions, such as "it is something you say when...," as CS in different communicative activities. Results showed that over 14 weeks of experiment, learners who received CS training outperformed those who did not receive CS instruction in speaking test scores and frequency of strategy use. Although combing conscious-raising technique with instruction appears to be a promising approach, these studies view the learning of CS as an individual task, putting more emphasis on how an individual constructs and applies the strategic knowledge.

However, there is a lack of studies that address the learning of CS from a socio constructivist perspective [9]. The use of peer feedback, for example, is a practice that can involve language learning through social interaction [6]. Theoretically, peer feedback is supported by Vygotskian sociocultural theory, which views learning as a socially constructed process [13]. The mechanism is that peer feedback creates reciprocal opportunities for learners at varying levels of skills and competence to work together and provide assistance to extend their competence [6]. A large volume of research in EFL writing has adopted peer feedback to support learners' writing process and found improvement in text revision and writing quality [5, 6, 11, 4]. However, to our best knowledge, there is very little research that uses peer feedback in EFL speaking. A study done by Huang (2010) is one of the few that examined the effect of group reflection on strategy use and oral language production. Although objective of the study was to compare the effects of different modalities of reflection, the design of group spoken reflection involved peer review mechanism to some extent. It was found that the group who practiced reflection as team work led to better CS use than the group who did not practice the reflection on CS. No difference found in the oral production between the two groups.

Different from many studies whose emphasis is on individual's learning of CS, this study aims to engage students in a reciprocal peer review process for learning the communication strategies and enhancing oral communication performance. Specifically, a mobile application Speaking Yo was designed to implement peer review inside the classroom. The use of peer feedback serves as a mediational means to allow learners to observe their speaking processes as well as receive meta-cognitive support from their peers. Two research questions guided the study:

1. Does providing peer feedback through Speaking Yo enhance communication performance?
2. Does providing peer feedback through Speaking Yo enhance the use of communication strategies?

3 Method

To examine the effects of peer feedback, a mobile application Speaking Yo was designed. A quasi-experiment was conducted using Speaking Yo in a Writing and Presentation course in a vocational university for four weeks. Since the course was discussion-based, Speaking Yo was used to engage students in the discussion tasks. Two classes of students were randomly assigned into an experimental group and a control group, which were taught by the same instructor. Both groups received instruction on CS and completed identical discussion tasks on Speaking Yo. Only the experimental group went through the peer review process.

3.1 Participants

Forty-five undergraduate students participated in the 4-week experiment. Five students were removed from the analysis because their pre- and post-tests were incomplete, leaving forty valid students, 20 for the experimental group and 20 for the control group. All of them were Mandarin speakers and had an average score of 630 ($SD = 89.30$) on TOEIC.

3.2 CS Selection and Peer Review Prompts

Three oral communication strategies, confirmation request, clarification requests and circumlocution, were based on guidelines proposed by [10] and the consultation with the course instructor. These CS were considered the crucial ones that students needed to participate in classroom discussion for the course. Three corresponding prompting questions were designed to elicit peer feedback (see Table 1). Regardless of their answers being yes or no to the prompting questions, students are required to further provide concrete CS-related examples from the replay of their conversation or give new CS-related suggestions.

Table 1. Communication strategy and peer review prompts

CS	Example	Prompting questions for peer review
Confirmation request	*You mean* he did not get my point?	Did your partner make sure that you understand what he/she wants to say?
Clarification requests	What do you mean?	Did your partner ask for an explanation when he/she didn't understand what you said?
Circumlocution	It is something that we use to dry our hands (Tissue).	Did your partner try to say in other words or describe when you didn't understand what he/she said?

3.3 Instruments

A conversation simulation task was adapted from [8] to examine the two dependent variables in this study: Communication strategy sue and oral communication performance. The task serves as both pre- and posttest. In the task, students were given a hypothetical situation and were instructed to prepare for a role play.

To measure the use of communication strategy, the oral production was first transcribed and then classified by two trained research assistants based on: (1) students' active behavior in repairing and maintaining the interaction [8] and (2) the three coding schemes, confirmation request, clarification requests and circumlocution taught in the course [10]. To measure oral communication performance, the oral production was rated by research assistants using Oral Communication Assessment Scale developed for EFL learners [8]. The scale consists of seven levels and focuses on the learner's fluency, ability to interact with the interlocutor, and flexibility in developing conversation.

3.4 System Architecture

Speaking Yo was developed in Java programming language using the Android software development kit. The application was used to engage students in classroom discussion and provide peer review mechanism. Four phases of learning sequence were designed on a weekly basis: (1) Introduction of weekly topics, (2) Discussion tasks, (3) Peer review on the conversation replay, and (4) Discussion/Reflection on peer feedback. Phase 1, 2 and 3 are embedded in Speaking Yo.

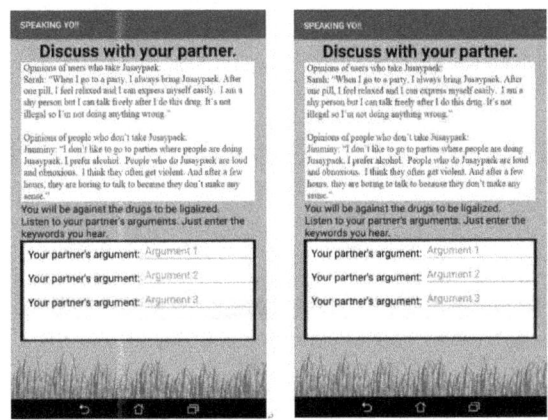

Fig. 1. Discussion tasks (Phase 2)

In Phase 2, the system prompts students to discuss the weekly topics and enter their responses on the smartphone as Fig. 1(a) shows. In Phase 3, which is the peer review phase, the system presents three prompting questions corresponding to the three target CS, prompts participants to listen to the replay of their previous discussion and then asks them to provide feedback as Fig. 2 shows. The replay of the discussion was mandatory but participants can drag the bar to fast forward.

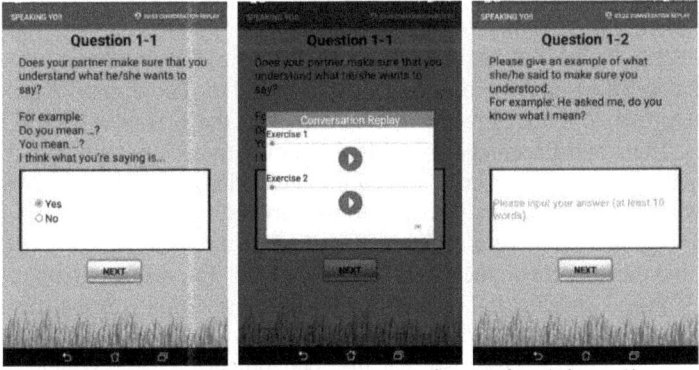

Fig. 2. Peer review on the conversation replay (Phase 3)

In Phase 4, which is the Discussion/Reflection phase, as Fig. 3 shows, the system immediately delivers the feedback to the peers and prompts them to discuss it. Finally, the system asks all the participants to reflect on their oral production and to rate the peer feedback. Upon completion, the system shows the total star points given by the partners.

Fig. 3. Discussion/Reflection on peer feedback (Phase 4)

3.5 Procedure

After the research team obtained students' consensus on participation, students received treatments according to the control and experimental groups assigned. In the first week, all participants took a conversation simulation task as the pretest for 15 minutes on the application, 5 minutes for the role play preparation and 10 minutes for the actual task. Then, they were familiarized with the learning activities and the operation of the application. Following that, they were given the instruction on how to use the target communication strategies and encouraged to use them throughout the experiment.

In the Week 2, 3 and 4, participants went through different phrases of learning activities depending on the group they were assigned to. Those in the experimental group were first introduced to the weekly topics in the first class for 50 minutes (Phase 1). Then, in the second class, as Fig. 4 shows, they were randomly paired up to carry out the Discussion tasks for 20 minutes (Phase 2). After the Discussion tasks were done, participants were asked to start the peer review for 20 minutes (Phase 3). Finally, they were asked to first discuss the feedback provided by the partners and then reflect on their own oral production. The control group did not go through Phrase 3 and Phase 4 as peer review and discussion was the treatment of the experiment. Note that the time for the Discussion tasks was prolonged to 50 minutes for the control group so that the total practice time was held constant. Finally, an additional of 20 minutes were added to week 4 for administering a post-test.

Fig. 4. Students using mobiles in the experimental group

4 Results

The first research question concerns whether providing peer feedback through Speaking Yo enhances communication performance. An ANCOVA was performed using oral scores on the pretest as covariate to examine the differences in the oral scores on the oral communication test between the two groups. To ensure that there is no interaction between the pretest scores and posttest scores, the assumption of homogeneity of regression slopes was tested and met. The results showed that, after controlling for the individual differences in communication ability, the experimental group (M = 4.45, SD = 0.759) outperformed the control group (M = 4.15, SD = 1.137) on the oral communication test, $F(1,37)$ = 7.331, p =.010, η^2 =.445, with a large effect size.

The results indicate that through peer feedback, participants' oral communication performance was enhanced. Both groups fall into level 4 on the scale of 7, suggesting that participants can communicate moderately effectively in the oral task [8]. With the oral scores being higher, those who received feedback may make less pauses, show more flexibility and maintain conversation in a more active way according to the descriptors of the task. It appears that pairing students with varying levels of speaking competence and skills can help them become aware of the weaknesses or their oral performance. Our system log showed that students' feedback included identification of speech errors and corrective input, such as pointing out that towel should not be pronounced as tower. Note that these types of feedback are not necessarily CS relevant.

The second research question concerns whether providing peer feedback through Speaking Yo enhances the use of the three target communication strategies. Three respective ANCOVAs, using pretest scores in CS use as covariate, were performed on the number of the three target CS on the posttest. The results showed that there is no significant difference between the two groups in the use of Confirmation request, $F(1,37) = .835$, $p = .367$, Circumlocution, $F(1,37) = .054$, $p = .817$ and Clarification request, $F(1,37) = 1.212$, $p = .278$.

The results indicate that the use of feedback did not lead to more CS use. It appears that the means of CS use in the current study, which range between 0.05 and 1.5, are relatively low when compared with the means reported by Nakatani [8], which range between 1.14 and 4.82. One possible explanation is that the peer review might have brought the target CS to learners' attention, but the peer feedback given was not concrete enough. Our observation from the system log supported this notion. It was found that under the Clarification request for example some learners provided non-linguistic feedback such as "*He speaks common English. He does it very well. I think he can be better.*" This type of feedback is referred to as rubber stamp advice [6, 12] because it does not directly address CS. This can be attributed to learners' lack of knowledge and skills [6].

5 Conclusion

This study is among the few to examine the effect of reciprocal peer review on the use of communication strategies and oral communication performance from a socio constructivist perspective. The design of the peer review embedded in Speaking Yo aims to provide opportunities for leaners to learn from their peers who vary in their oral skills and competence as well as to become aware of their use of communication strategies. The results showed that the use of peer feedback enhanced students' oral communication performance over a short period of four weeks. However, it did not improve the use of communication strategies. The findings suggest that Speaking Yo enables learners to monitor their oral production and to provide/receive corrective feedback on their overall communication ability. However, the feedback provided by the peers was not concrete enough to address the use of communication strategies. Future research should look into how learners can be scaffolded to better provide concrete and useful feedback when carrying out peer review. It will also be beneficial to explore the effects of pairing learners with peers that are at a similar or different levels of language competence as a way to optimize the peer review.

6 Acknowledgements

This research was supported by the National Science Council, Taiwan under project numbers MOST106-2511-S-110 -002 -MY3, MOST104-2511-S-110 -009 -MY3 and MOST104-2511-S-110 -007 -MY3.

7 References

[1] Ellis, R. (1984). Communication strategies and the evaluation of communicative performance. *ELT Journal, 38*(1), 39-44. doi: 10.1093/elt/38.1.39

[2] Faerch, C., & Kasper, G. (1986). Strategic competence in foreign language teaching. *Learning, teaching and communication in the foreign language classroom*, 179-193.

[3] Huang, L.-S. (2010). Do different modalities of reflection matter? An exploration of adult second-language learners' reported strategy use and oral language production. *System, 38*(2), 245-261. doi: https://doi.org/10.1016/j.system.2010.03.005

[4] Long, M. H. (1983). Native speaker/non-native speaker conversation and the negotiation of comprehensible input1. *Applied Linguistics, 4*(2), 126-141. doi: 10.1093/applin/4.2.126

[5] Lundstrom, K., & Baker, W. (2009). To give is better than to receive: The benefits of peer review to the reviewer's own writing. *Journal of Second Language Writing, 18*(1), 30-43. doi: https://doi.org/10.1016/j.jslw.2008.06.002

[6] Min, H.-T. (2005). Training students to become successful peer reviewers. *System, 33*(2), 293-308. doi: https://doi.org/10.1016/j.system.2004.11.003

[7] Nakatani, Y. (2005). The Effects of Awareness-Raising Training on Oral Communication Strategy Use. *The Modern Language Journal, 89*(1), 76-91. doi: 10.1111/j.0026-7902.2005.00266.x

[8] Nakatani, Y. (2010). Identifying Strategies That Facilitate EFL Learners' Oral Communication: A Classroom Study Using Multiple Data Collection Procedures. *The Modern Language Journal, 94*(1), 116-136. doi: 10.1111/j.1540-4781.2009.00987.x

[9] Nguyen, M. H. (2013). EFL Students' Reflections on Peer Scaffolding in Making a Collaborative Oral Presentation. *English Language Teaching, 6*(4), 64-73.

[10] Rabab'ah, G. (2016). The Effect of Communication Strategy Training on the Development of EFL Learners' Strategic Competence and Oral Communicative Ability. *Journal of Psycholinguistic Research, 45*(3), 625-651. doi: 10.1007/s10936-015-9365-3

[11] Storch, N. (2005). Collaborative writing: Product, process, and students' reflections. *Journal of Second Language Writing, 14*(3), 153-173.

[12] Tsui, A. B. M., & Ng, M. (2000). Do Secondary L2 Writers Benefit from Peer Comments? *Journal of Second Language Writing, 9*(2), 147-170. doi: https://doi.org/10.1016/S1060-3743(00)00022-9

[13] Vygotsky, L. (1978). Interaction between learning and development. *Readings on the development of children, 23*(3), 34-41.

[14] Yang, Y.-F. (2011). A reciprocal peer review system to support college students' writing. *British Journal of Educational Technology, 42*(4), 687-700. doi: 10.1111/j.1467-8535.2010.01059.x

Exploring General Morphological Analysis and Providing Personalized Recommendations to Stimulate Creativity with *ReaderBench*

Daniela Stamati[1], Maria-Dorinela Sirbu[1], Mihai Dascalu[1,2], Stefan Trausan-Matu[1,2]

[1] University Politehnica of Bucharest, 313 Splaiul Independenței, 060042, Bucharest, Romania
{daniela.stamati, maria.sirbu}@cti.pub.ro,
{mihai.dascalu, stefan.trausan}@cs.pub.ro
[2] Academy of Romanian Scientists, 54 Splaiul Independenței, 050094, Bucharest, Romania

Abstract. Computer Supported Collaborative Learning (CSCL) has gained a steadily increasing role as it helps students to better comprehend through its synergistic effect, mediated by technology. In line with CSCL learning paradigm, our approach is centered on creativity stimulation which is facilitated by a deeper understanding of the dialog. This paper introduces new extended views for our *ReaderBench* framework, as well as a novel recommendations engine. Our General Morphological Analysis (GMA) implementation is based on the keywords extraction mechanism provided by *ReaderBench*, alongside with the similar concepts inferred using the lexicalized ontology WordNet, Latent Semantic Analysis (LSA), and Latent Dirichlet Analysis (LDA) semantic models. We also include a comprehensive case study to detail the new processing workflows that integrate voices (i.e., participants' points of view), keywords identification, and text cohesion in order to recommend personalized learning resources.

Keywords: Creativity stimulation; General Morphological Analysis; Dialogism; Semantic models; Personalized recommendations of learning resources; *ReaderBench* framework.

1 Introduction

Learning entails the acquisition of knowledge on specific topics and the process can be enhanced by relying on trending technologies and paradigms. Computer Supported Collaborative Learning (CSCL) helps students to build knowledge and understand more easily, achieve a common purpose, support each other for better understanding, and improve their communication skills [1]. While considering creativity stimulation, it is important that, by using online conversations for learning, students share different knowledge and experiences to generate new ideas and points of view, while being from different geographical areas can be an additional advantage. In this way, participants encounter different points of view and can share their experiences with others. Using divergent and convergent thinking, students are able to share their ideas and to learn in a structured way [2].

Dialogism, derived from Bakhtin's work [3], is considered a framing for CSCL. It takes into account different 'voices' (i.e., points of view uttered by participants or ideas, operationalized as semantic chains of related concepts [4, 5]) in order to provide an in-depth analysis of discourse. As Bakhtin [3] wrote, multiple voices interanimate and impact one another in a polyphonic manner, similar to the music case. Dialogism and polyphony, as its high order manifestation, represent a way to stimulate creativity [6, 7]. Besides dialogism, of particular interest to the problem at hand is General Morphological Analysis (GMA) [8, 9] that represents a multidimensional problem solving technique. Our approach analyzes a chat conversation by determinating which voice (point of view) dominates the discussion and how voices interact one with another, i.e. inter-animate. This study represents a continuation of the experiments performed by Oprisan and Trausan-Matu [10] and Stamati, Dascalu and Trausan-Matu [11] and it includes new visualizations, as well as a recommendations engine later on presented in detail.

The next section introduces the central theoretical concepts used in our analysis, as well as GMA as a model for stimulating creativity. Section three presents an overview of our *ReaderBench* framework [12, 13], as well as the dedicated user interfaces to visualize voices. Section four is focused on extending the GMA model in order to provide recommendations of learning resources from Wikipedia, followed by conclusions.

2 Theoretical Overview grounded in CSCL

Computer Supported Collaborative Learning (CSCL) refers to a learning activity based on social interactions, facilitated or mediated by computers and technology [1, 14]. Collaborative learning, in general, refers to a series of educational practices that involve a common effort of students to solve a problem or assimilate new knowledge. Among learners, the role of the teacher is more supervisory- or mediation-oriented, encouraging the transfer of ideas among students. Unlike cooperation in which students are responsible for a sub-problem from the overarching task, collaborative learning is centered on the synergistic effect of concurrently achieving a common purpose, at the same time. Although there may be portions in the collaborative process in which cooperation appears, this is not planned from the beginning [15].

In addition, it is important to consider people who have different knowledge and, more than that, different experiences when defining the study groups. A great contribution to collaborative learning is given by contradictory arguments because they catalyze a cognitive effort and encourage both the research of different ideas, as well as the reasoned argumentation of a point of view. Vygotsky and Piaget [16] conducted an initial series of collaborative learning studies. Vygotsky supports the involvement of a teacher or an adult in the learning process while considering that the optimal area lies between what students can learn by themselves, and what they can learn with the help of a more competent person. Piaget further develops this theory and emphasizes that the study group should be heterogeneous and that the participants should have different knowledge for an optimal collaboration [16].

2.1 Divergent and Convergent Thinking. Dialogical Polyphony to Stimulate Creativity

The human mind can be perceived as containing a knowledge network that evolves through the subsequent integration of new information, during both personal and social knowledge-building processes [17]. The way new ideas arise is highly dependent on the architecture of this network and how the central concepts are connected one to another. An idea is connected to the entire knowledge network that is put together in order to generate a broad definition around the idea, during a four stage process that includes preparation, incubation, lighting and verification [18].

Divergent and convergent thinking are the main two processes that support the generation of new ideas [2]. Divergent thinking can draw inspiration from alternative sources and brings more solutions to the same problem. In contrast, convergent thinking is a structured approach that relies on facts and brings only one solution to a problem. Both types of thinking play an important role, both for generating ideas at the individual level, and for introducing ideas in a collaborative learning setting.

Dialogism is considered the framing paradigm for CSCL [19] as it provides the grounds for building a comprehensive model of discourse, while relating to multiple perspectives pertaining to different speakers. Bakhtin [3] analyzed how multiple voices coexist and influence one another in a polyphonic manner within the same context, in novels. A monophonic world in Bakhtin's vision is made up of a single isolated topic. No theme from a monophonic discourse produces a secondary meaning and the discourse converges to a truth considered absolute that leaves no room for debate. In contrast, dialogism considers additional perspectives and voices. In dialogue, voices interact, evolve and influence each other, potentially being merged, thus creating a collective perception of truth generated from the dialogic interactions between individuals. A voice is an idea that lives through participants, but is independent of them and has no time constraints. Moreover, dialogism can exist in any type of text while voices become recurrent topics or themes emerging from the discourse.

Similar to the rules of *counterpoint* from musical theory, the interaction of seemingly divergent (dissonant) voices ultimately converge towards harmony [4, 5]. This dissonance catalyzes creativity [6, 7], as voices are challenged by other points of view. Thus, multiple perspectives or voices are precisely the constituent required to stimulate and obtain creativity in a collaborative learning setting.

2.2 General Morphological Analysis

General Morphological Analysis (GMA) [8, 9] is a multidimensional problem solving technique that explores all possible solutions for complex, non-quantified inputs. The method was initially developed by Zwicky [20] and applied for the first time in the study of astronomy. Afterwards, it was extended and applied into multiple domains, including engineering and technology, policy analysis or organizational development. The underlying process starts with an abstraction of parameters, their transposition into an *n*-dimensional matrix consisting of morphological boxes (i.e., "Zwicky box"), followed by a cross consistency assessment of configurations. GMA provides reliable results when the input set is large; however, in this case we cannot perform a manual analysis of the problem space and of all its variables. One of the most important challenges of the algorithm is the quantification of complex problems into discrete inputs, given that the considered problems potentially contain social, political and cognitive dimensions.

3   The *ReaderBench* Framework

ReaderBench [12, 13] is a discourse analysis framework relying on advanced Natural Language Processing techniques designed to assist teachers in assessing how students learn and comprehend. Our assessments are centered on three pillars: a) assessing textual complexity centered on cohesion, which is computationally quantified in terms of semantic similarity between text segments, b) the identification of reading strategies, and c) the evaluation of participation and collaboration in CSCL environments [21], including an implementation of the polyphonic model of discourse [4] which is inspired from dialogism. The processing pipeline integrates the automated identification of voices operationalized as semantic chains of related words, keywords mining, and assessment of text cohesion in order to facilitate a visual representation of voices (see Figures 1 and 2). This also facilities the follow-up personalized recommendations that are provided in order to stimulate creativity.

Our GMA implementation is based on the keywords extraction mechanism provided by *ReaderBench* that represents the inputs of our approach, alongside similar concepts inferred using the lexicalized ontology WordNet, Latent Semantic Analysis (LSA) and Latent Dirichlet Analysis (LDA) [12]. The newly introduced visualizations can assist in analyzing a series of chat features such as its homogeneity, the linkage between voices and emerging co-occurrence patterns, as well as participants' degree of involvement in relation to specific themes or voices. For all presented graphical representations, only the most prevalent three voices were selected, each voice being depicted as a triple of the first three most representative underlying words (see Table 1 for sample voices used in subsequent views, including the number of constituent words and the colors used for rendering).

Table 1. Voice samples.

Voice	# words	Color
(answer, information, say)	278	yellow
(use, product, think)	254	green
(blog, talk, read)	162	violet

In dialogism, *echoes* [5] are defined as the phenomenon of voice propagation throughout the discourse. In Figure 1 we observe how participant 4 started talking about the disadvantages of a chat environment, while participants 1 and 3 supported this point of view with several arguments. The echo is not limited in time, as an echo may appear long after a voice is emitted, even as a result of a different conversation.

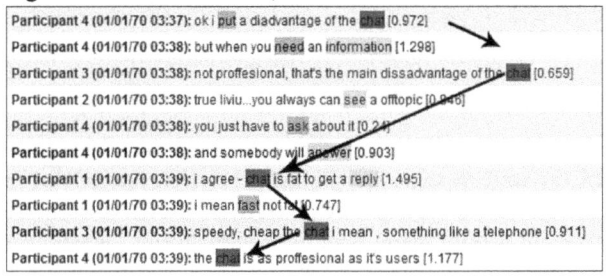

Fig. 1. Echo visualization in *ReaderBench*.

Ventriloquism [6] consists of the process in which a voice is taken over by another participant and we must emphasize that this process can also include the altering of the voice. Participants perceive a voice in their own way, they can accept or reject a certain point of view; nevertheless, the voice is adapted to each participant's personal vision. Figure 2 depicts an example of ventriloquism; after participant 1 has exemplified a communication and documentary tool in a company - i.e., the blog -, participants 3 and 4 also give other examples of tools that are used in companies, namely wiki pages and chats.

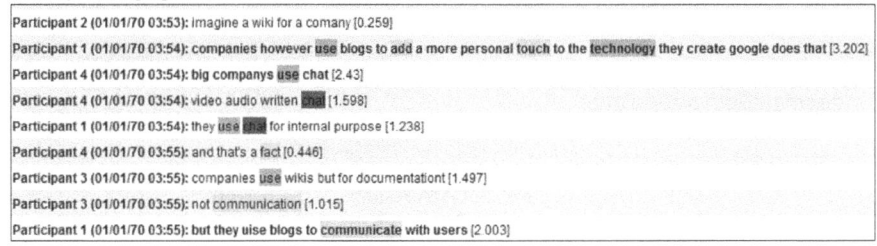

Fig. 2. Ventriloquism example.

The highlighting of voices which was introduced in this paper, alongside an implementation of GMA in *ReaderBench*, facilitates the monitoring and analysis of conversations. Users can easily observe which voices dominated the discussion, how they inter-animated one with another, and how these voices generated subsequent echoes or became instances of ventriloquism.

4 Extended Case Study Centered on Providing Personalized Recommendations

The envisioned creativity task presented in this paper is centered on the evaluation of multiparticipant chat conversations. The considered sample conversation was selected from a collection of more than 50 chats in which 4th year undergraduate students from our university debated on the advantage and disadvantages of certain CSCL technologies. The selected chat exhibits an off-balanced participation among its members, thus better highlighting the benefits of suggesting external learning resources.

4.1 Personalized Recommendations

The generated personalized recommendations of additional lecture resources are based on GMA, as well as semantic similarity between the articles retrieved from Wikipedia and the topics discussed in conversation, presented in descending order. The recommendation service starts with each participant's keywords and identifies similar concepts using LSA, LDA and WordNet. The participant's keywords are automatically extracted from conversations and a corresponding relevance score is computed expressing statistical presence and semantic relatedness [22]. Similar concepts are identified as the *k* nearest neighbors of the identified keywords using each semantic space individually; afterwards, the average semantic similarity score is used to rank inferred concepts based on their relatedness. As an example, the input set of words from Figure 3 for GMA was made up of the concepts "blog", "company", and "forum". For each of these concepts, a set of semantically similar concepts was determined. While selecting the "blog" and "forum" words, we can see how the algorithm determined that these concepts relate to "society" from the "company" dimension: the sematic relatedness values between "society"–"blog", respectively "society"–"forum", exceed an imposed similarity threshold.

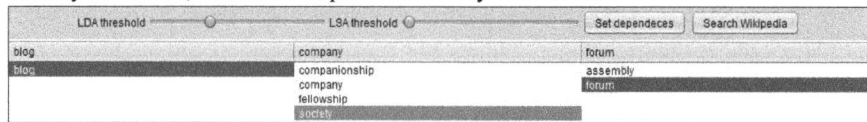

LDA threshold	LSA threshold	Set dependeces	Search Wikipedia
blog	company	forum	
blog	companionship	assembly	
	company	forum	
	fellowship		
	society		

Fig. 3. GMA results.

The next step consists of performing Wikipedia queries using the CirrusSearch API (https://www.mediawiki.org/wiki/Extension:CirrusSearch), the selected words (i.e., "blog" and "forum"), as well as a combination of these concepts alongside with the recommendations provided by GMA. Therefore, for this particular case, five searches were launched: {"blog"}, {"forum"}, {"blog", "society"}, {"forum", "society"}, {"blog", "forum", "society"}. In order to stimulate chat creativity, personalized suggestions for specific external articles were added in blocking conditions. For this study, we considered that the discussion was blocked if the participants did not talk for at least five minutes.

4.2 Extending GMA with Dialogism

Time breaks of more than five minutes divide the discourse into several sections and our aim is to deliver appropriate content for each of these sections. The implemented approach relies on voices; more specifically, the algorithm suggests relevant articles for each section based on the predominant voice. Exploring a voice with GMA is performed by taking into account the key concepts from the voice which have a high cohesion score with the discussion. Therefore, only the concepts from the intersection between the most discussed concepts from the conversation and the most central ones in terms of cohesion were chosen as input for GMA. This approach provides a series of alternative directions while relating to the explored voice.

As follow-up, we analyzed the degree of involvement of each participant within the discussion. First, we extracted the keywords from the conversation (see Table 2 in which the relevance score is a global measure of significance computed using the *ReaderBench* framework [22]).

Table 2. Central conversation keywords.

keyword (1)	relevance	keyword (2)	relevance	keyword (3)	relevance
blog	16.64	information	6.56	write	6.01
add	7.78	read	6.43	give	5.26
product	7.5	company	6.33	post	4.97
tell	7.34	answer	6.07	take	4.54

Second, in order to stimulate creativity on skipped concepts, we determined the keywords that were *not* used by a certain participant (see Table 3 for omitted words). We can observe a tight correlation with Figure 4 that depicts the cumulative participation evolution for each member: the evolution of the second participant is lower when compared to other participants as (s)he approached fewer topics. However, slower overall evolutions or lower global participation scores can also relate to participants' degree of sociability, not necessarily to their knowledge level.

Table 3. Omitted keywords not used by each chat participant.

Participant	Keywords
Participant 1	answer, write, give, communication
Participant 2	add, information, read, give, post, talk, communication, blog, time
Participant 3	product, tell, read, take, technology, blog
Participant 4	add, read, question, communication, blog

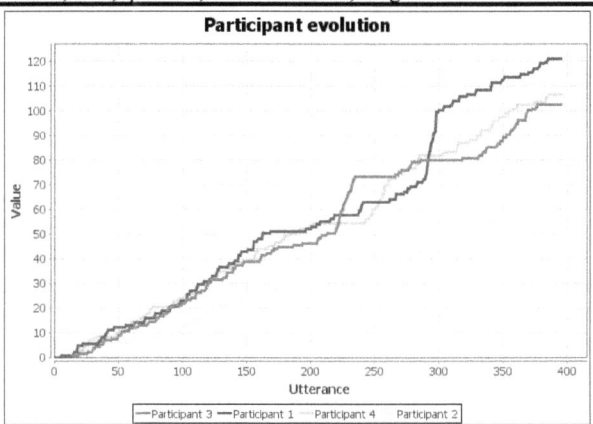

Fig. 4. Participants' evolution determined using the *ReaderBench* framework.

Third, we filter the omitted keywords by specificity and relevance in order to avoid querying after general words (such as "add", "read" or "question") or words with a low impact on the overall discourse. The thresholds imposed after incremental experiments include: a) a minimum depth of 5 within the WordNet taxonomy and b) a minimum relevance of 6.5 (see Table 4 for suggested keywords in terms of creativity stimulation).

Table 4. Suggested keywords for creativity.

Participant	Keyword	Relevance	Depth
Participant 1	answer	6.07	5
Participant 2	post	5.00	7
Participant 3	product	7.50	6
Participant 4	-	-	-

Fourth, a personalized search was performed for each participant after determining the number of times each student referred to one of the keywords suggested by the teacher (see Table 5). The values in bold reflect the maximum for each concept and we can observe that each participant was the advocate for a specific technology. The relevance scores for the "wiki" keyword could not be computed as the concept was not present in the considered semantic models from *ReaderBench*.

Table 5. Incidence of imposed keywords.

	forum		wiki		blog		chat	
	TF	Rel.	TF	Rel.	TF	Rel.	TF	Rel.
Participant 1	8	1.77	4	-	**36**	**2.80**	5	1.23
Participant 2	2	1.34	**14**	-	4	2.46	3	0.98
Participant 3	**17**	**1.73**	8	-	8	2.36	12	0.70
Participant 4	8	1.75	4	-	8	2.49	**15**	**1.36**

Fifth, we provide personalized recommendations by selecting words that have the potential to be less known – i.e., either specific words omitted by the participant, or imposed keywords that were not addressed. Thus, our recommendations engine suggests articles from Wikipedia that have been less discussed by the participants during the discussion (see Figure 5).

5 Conclusions

Computer Supported Collaborative Learning helps students learn by socializing, sharing opinions, giving advices and supporting others to understand a problem or the corresponding solution. This paper represents a continuation of the study performed by Stamati, Dascalu and Trausan-Matu [11] and it includes new extended views, as well as a novel recommendations engine. Our approach is based on GMA and is centered on creativity stimulation, corroborated with a deeper understanding of the conversation. The paper also includes a comprehensive case study used to highlight the new workflows that have a wide applicability in terms of suggesting learning resources.

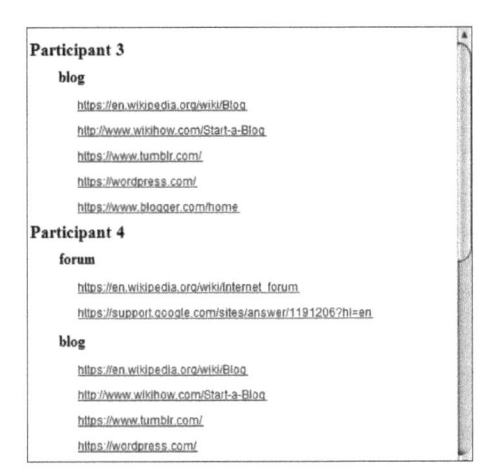

Fig. 5. Suggested articles.

Starting from the GMA implementation which was based on keywords extraction mechanisms provided by *ReaderBench*, this paper presents an evaluation of multiparticipant chat conversations, namely: which voices dominated the discussion, how voices inter-animated one with another, and how these voices generated subsequent echoes or became instances of ventriloquism. Based on the GMA results, we generated personalized recommendations for each participant using semantic similarity between articles retrieved from Wikipedia and the discussed topics.

Nevertheless, we must present the limitations of our approach. First, the central words to be used in GMA need to be manually selected by the user. Second, words need to be properly represented within our semantic models (e.g., "wiki" which was disregarded). Third, we also rely on the list of keywords imposed by the teacher which were manually coded for this analysis. These words represent clear concepts to be covered; in their absence, we are obliged to rely only on the emerging keywords of the conversation and, in case of off-topics discussions, our system could provide external resources with reduced educational value.

Acknowledgements. This research was partially supported by the 644187 EC H2020 *Realising an Applied Gaming Eco-system* (RAGE) project, as well as by the FP7 2008-212578 LTfLL project.

References

1. Stahl, G.: Group cognition. Computer support for building collaborative knowledge. MIT Press, Cambridge, MA (2006)
2. Vohs, K.D., Baumeister, R.F. (eds.): Handbook of Self-Regulation: Research, theory, and applications. The Guildford Press, New York, NY & London (2011)

3. Bakhtin, M.M.: Problems of Dostoevsky's poetics. University of Minnesota Press, Minneapolis (1984)
4. Trausan-Matu, S., Stahl, G., Sarmiento, J.: Polyphonic Support for Collaborative Learning. In: Groupware: Design, Implementation, and Use, 12th International Workshop (CRIWG 2006), Vol. LNCS 4154, pp. 132–139. Springer, Medina del Campo, Spain (2006)
5. Trausan-Matu, S.: A Polyphonic Model, Analysis Method and Computer Support Tools for the Analysis of Socially-Built Discourse. Romanian Journal of Information Science and Technology, 16(2-3), 144–154 (2013)
6. Trausan-Matu, S.: Un model polifonic pentru creativitatea în grupurile colaborative virtuale de mici dimensiuni. Revista Romana de Interactiune Om-Calculator, 6(1), 57–78 (2013)
7. Trausan-Matu, S.: Computer support for creativity in small groups using chats. Annals of the Academy of Romanian Scientists, Series on Science and Technology of Information, 3(2), 81–90 (2010)
8. Ritchey, T.: General Morphological Analysis: A general method for non-quantified modeling. Swedish Morphological Society (1998)
9. Ritchey, T.: Wicked problems–social messes: Decision support modelling with morphological analysis, Vol. 17. Springer Science & Business Media (2011)
10. Oprisan, A., Trausan-Matu, S.: Creativity Stimulation Tool. Annals of the Academy of Romanian Scientists, Series on Science and Technology of Information, 6(1), 63–83 (2013)
11. Stamati, D., Dascalu, M., Trausan-Matu, S.: Creativity stimulation in chat conversations through morphological analysis. University Politehnica of Bucharest Scientific Bulletin Series C-Electrical Engineering and Computer Science, 77(4), 17–30 (2015)
12. Dascalu, M.: Analyzing discourse and text complexity for learning and collaborating, Studies in Computational Intelligence, Vol. 534. Springer, Cham, Switzerland (2014)
13. Dascalu, M., Dessus, P., Bianco, M., Trausan-Matu, S., Nardy, A.: Mining texts, learner productions and strategies with ReaderBench. In: Peña-Ayala, A. (ed.) Educational Data Mining: Applications and Trends, pp. 345–377. Springer, Cham, Switzerland (2014)
14. Stahl, G., Koschmann, T., Suthers, D.: Computer-supported collaborative learning: An historical perspective. In: Sawyer, R.K. (ed.) Cambridge handbook of the learning sciences, pp. 409–426. Cambridge University Press, Cambridge, UK (2006)
15. Lai, E.R.: Collaboration: A Literature Review. Pearson: Research Reports (2011) 48
16. Dillenbourg, P., Baker, M., Blaye, A., O'Malley, C.: The evolution of research on collaborative learning. In: Spada, E., Reiman, P. (eds.) Learning in Humans and Machine: Towards an interdisciplinary learning science. Elsevier, Oxford (1996)
17. Bereiter, C.: Education and mind in the knowledge age. Lawrence Erlbaum Associates, Mahwah, NJ (2002)
18. Wallas, G.: The Art of Thought: Graham Wallas on the Four Stages of Creativity. (1926)
19. Koschmann, T.: Toward a dialogic theory of learning: Bakhtin's contribution to understanding learning in settings of collaboration. In: Int. Conf. on Computer Support for Collaborative Learning (CSCL'99), pp. 308–313. ISLS, Palo Alto (1999)
20. Zwicky, F.: Discovery, Invention, Research - Through the Morphological Approach. The Macmillian Company, Toronto (1969)
21. Dascalu, M., Trausan-Matu, S., McNamara, D.S., Dessus, P.: ReaderBench – Automated Evaluation of Collaboration based on Cohesion and Dialogism. International Journal of Computer-Supported Collaborative Learning, 10(4), 395–423 (2015)
22. Dascalu, M., McNamara, D.S., Trausan-Matu, S., Allen, L.K.: Cohesion Network Analysis of CSCL Participation. Behavior Research Methods, 1–16 (2017)

Higher Cognitive Items Generation Algorithms

Ebenezer Aggrey[1], Maiga Chang[1], Rita Kuo[2], and Xiaokun Zhang[1]

[1] School of Computing and Information Systems, Athabasca University, Canada
[2] Department of Computer Science and Engineering, New Mexico institute of Mining and Technology, USA
aggreyeb@shaw.ca, rita.mcsl@gmail.com, maiga@ms2.hinet.net, xiaokunz@athabascau.ca

Abstract. The main goal of this research is to design item generation algorithms which can be integrated into the Online Test System developed earlier by the authors. The algorithms will be capable of generating items belong to higher cognitive level based on Bloom Taxonomy from a knowledge map created by a teacher (or co-created by a group of teachers). With the help of such integrated system teachers can reduce the time and effort they spend to prepare tests for assessing students' mastery and understanding level of what they taught in class. This paper discusses the proposed algorithms in details and explains the experiment design in the end.

Keywords: Knowledge Map. Item Generation. Hierarchical Concept Map. Concept Schema. Test Items generation Algorithms.

1. Introduction

Data structure is one of the foundation courses which is widely taught in science and engineering in many higher institutions. Chris, is a teacher who teaches undergraduate computer science. He taught his class data structure interfaces and their implementations concepts and wished to use the data structure concept hierarchy he presented to prepare higher and lower cognitive multiple choice test items to assess his students' cognitive abilities.

So what did Chris do? He spent days and a lot of efforts to prepare the test items and mark students' answer sheets manually, then he wondered whether or not there is a way to generate the test items from the data structure concepts and to mark students' answer sheets automatically. The answer is Yes, many researchers in literature have used different techniques: template-based [4], Natural Language Processing-based [6], and Knowledge map-based [7], to develop automatic item generation systems with the aim to reduce the time and effort that Chris and other teachers may need to spend on preparing test items. However, most of these systems can only generate items for lower cognitive levels.

The purpose of this research is to design item generation algorithms for existing Online Test System (OTS) research which allows teachers to create knowledge map for their own course and manage tests for their students. The research makes the OTS capable of generating items for both lower and higher cognitive level automatically based on the knowledge maps the teachers created. With the proposed algorithms' help, teachers will be able to generate items as their item bank for creating different tests with few effort.

The rest of this paper is organized as follows. Section 2 reviews the relevant literature for models applied in this research. Section 3 analyzes the conceptual model such as the Knowledge Map, Test item model. In addition, the general algorithm architecture will be presented in this section. In Section 4 the data to be used as inputs of the item generation algorithms and the algorithm design will be explained. Furthermore, the example demonstrating how major and minor algorithms working together to generate the items with outputs will be presented and explained. Section 5 explains the evaluation plan this research intend to verify the usability of the Online Test System and the effectiveness of the item generation algorithms in terms of whether or not the cognitive level each generated item belongs to is expected. Finally, Section 6 summarizes the research and discusses future works that can done later.

2. Relevant Research

Template-based [1, 11] and Knowledge Map approach [2, 7] are some of the techniques reported in literature to generate multiple choice items. While most of these approaches can generate items for lower cognitive levels and aims to assist teachers to reduce the time and effort they use to prepare test items, they cannot generate higher cognitive items. However, Template-based approach is cost effective in the sense that it can be uses to generate large amount test items by manipulating stimulus, stem, and options placeholder only. Moreover, common errors in developing multiple choice item such as omissions and additions of words, phrases, spelling, punctuations, capitalization, item structure, typeface, formatting can be avoided [5] because only the stimulus, stem, and options of the questions are being changed during question generation [10].

On the other hand Knowledge map approach has the ability to store additional information about the concept under consideration in its concept schema [2, 3] hence it can assist in the generation of higher cognitive items. This research investigate how to generate items for both higher and lower cognitive level from a knowledge map of Data Structure in the computer science domain.

3. Analysis

In order to define the specification for the item generation algorithms the research team performed the following iterative system analysis tasks.

3.1 Selecting Taxonomy to classify the items to be generated

The items to be generated has to be classified as higher or lower cognitive levels hence Blooms Taxonomy [8] was selected. It provides a useful guidelines to classify knowledge as well as cognitive processes to demonstrate learning. Many researchers in literature have leveraged it successfully to evaluate cognitive abilities of students and also prepare learning objectives [2].

Blooms Taxonomy uses verbs "Remember", "Understand" to signify lower cognitive process and "Apply", "Analyze", "Evaluate" as higher cognitive activities. Whiles lower cognitive process expects students to recall facts about concepts and classify concepts based on their characteristics and behavior, higher cognitive activities expect students to know how a concept under consideration works in real world situation. In context of Data Structure in computer science domain, for example given application of specific data structure the student will be able to select the suitable data structure for that particular task. Another example will be given a software components which utilizes the same data structure with their respective time complexity or order of growth of the implemented algorithms students will be able to select the best software component if running time is required specification or the memory usage is concern.

3.2 Selecting Knowledge Structure and defining conceptual model

For teachers to create and manage the knowledge structure – a conceptual model which defines the concepts and their properties, relationships, and constraints has to be develop. The research selected knowledge map for this task. Knowledge Map is a graphical representation of knowledge. Conceptually, it consist of two parts namely concept hierarchy and concept schema. Whiles the concept hierarchy presents the relations between concepts of interests, the concept schema store related information associated with the concepts [7]. Fig. 1 shows an example of concept hierarchy for the interface and its implementation in Data Structure course.

```
☐ Data Structure
    ☐ Linear
        ☐ Stack
        ☐ Queue
        ☐ Deque
        ☐ Linked-List
    ☐ None Linear
        ☐ Tree
        ☐ Graph
        ☐ Dictionary
        ☐ Heap
```

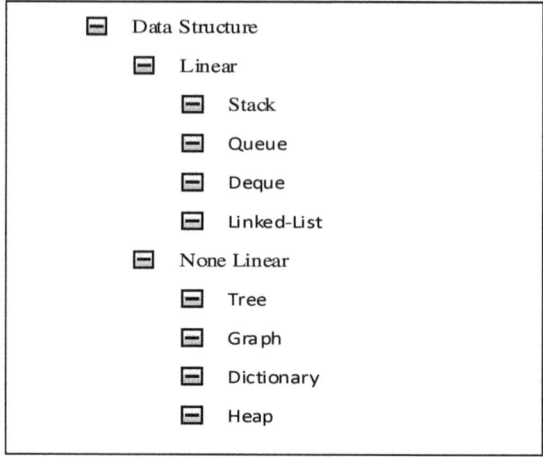

Fig. 1. A concept hierarchy example

The concepts are organized in a tree like structure. The root node is "Data Structure" and Linear and none linear are type of data structure. Stack, Queue, Deque, Linked-List are type of linear data structure and Tree, Graph, Dictionary, and Heap are type of None Linear data structure.

Formally, Knowledge Map is defined as KM = (H, S) where H is concept hierarchy and S is its concept schema. Concept hierarchy is a 3- tuple defined as H = (D, R, K) where D = {d1, d2..., dn} is a set of domain concepts, R = {r1, r2..., rn} is a set of relation between concepts and their parent. e.g. {"Type of", "Part of"}, and K = {k1, k2..., kn} is a set of constraints that should hold to create the concept or relations to be established.

Constraints for concept hierarchy are: IF H is a concept hierarchy THEN (1) H should have special node n, called Root with no parent node. (2) Each node referred in this research as Concept Node (N) such that N ≠ n has a unique parent node. And, (3) each concept node may have concept schema. It can inherit concept schema from parent node.

Concept schema stores additional information (i.e. relation name, concept name, concept action, attribute name, and attribute value). An example partial concept schemas for linear data structure is shown in table 4.

3.3 Defining conceptual model for Item

In this research an item consist of (1) stimulus which can be text or code segment that gives context to the question to being asked, (2) stem which is a question based on the stimulus, (3) answer options which consist of distractors, i.e. incorrect answers, (4) correct answer also known as the key, and, (5) cognitive type. There are four constraints for creating an item: (1) each item must have a stimulus; (2) each item must have a stem; (3) each item must have at least two answer options and up to four; and, (4) each item must have one correct answer.

For example a typical test item and it components (stimulus, stem, answer options are shown table 1.

Table 1. Typical Apply Cognitive type items

Cognitive Type	Stimulus	Stem	Answer Options
Apply	A programmer was asked to implement Stack data structure to be used for software component that simulate Last In First Out mechanism (LIFO).	Select the suitable functions the programmer has to implement	A. Push ,pop, peek B. peek ,enqueue, dequeue C. addFirst ,addLast, removeFirst D. add ,remove, contains
Apply	A student designed and implemented data structure for software module. Upon uniting testing it was found that the data structure exhibit Last In First Out mechanism (LIFO).	Choose the possible data structure the student implemented.	A. Queue B. Stack C. Deque D. Linked-List

3.4 Designing Item Algorithm Workflow

Figure 5 shows the workflow of item generation algorithm. The workflow has seven steps described as following in details:

1. A teacher can select cognitive type and a concept node. In this case the teacher wants the system to generate items for cognitive type Apply hence he or she choose cognitive type ct_A from the list and concept node c_t from the concept hierarchy. The selections then are sent as inputs of the "Algorithm Selection" function as Step 1 shows.

2. When "Algorithm Selection" function receives the chosen concept node and cognitive type, it select appropriate proper major algorithm accordingly. Since ct_A is received, the "Apply Item Generation" Algorithm is activated (as Step 2 shows) and the c_t and ct_A are passed into it as inputs.

3. The "Apply Item Generation" Algorithm uses ct_A to retrieve item rules of cognitive type Apply (R^A) as Step 3 shows.

4. After the algorithm gets R^A, it enters into a loop enumerating through the rules and perform the following tasks sequentially:

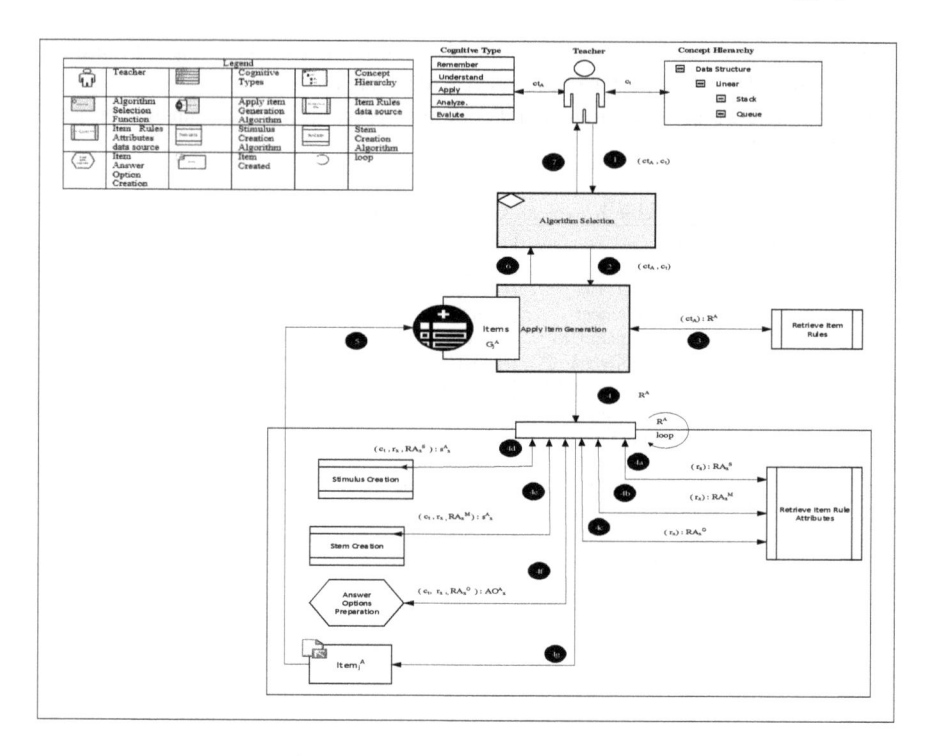

Fig. 5. Apply item algorithm workflow

(4a) Request for stimulus rule attributes (RA_x^S) passing the current rule (r_x) as parameter

(4b) Request stem rule attributes (RA_x^M) passing the current rule (r_x) as parameter

(4c) Request answer options rule attributes (RA_x^O) passing the current rule (r_x) as parameter

(4d) Ask "Stimulus Creation" supporting algorithm to create the item stimulus (s^A_x) by passing cognitive type c_t, a rule r_x, and the retrieved stimulus rule attributes set RA_x^S.

(4e) Execute "Stem Creation Algorithm" to create the item stem (m^A_x) passing c_t, current rule (r_x) and RA_x^M.

(4f) Call "Answer Options Preparation Algorithm" to prepare answer options and their key (AO^A_x) passing c_t, current rule (r_x), RA_x^O.

(4g) Create an item G with the outputs of Steps 4d to 4f, {s^A_x, m^A_x, AO^A_x} and add to the item generated set I as shown in Step 5.

5. In the end the "Apply Item Generation" algorithm passes back the generated item set G to the caller (as Step 6 shows) and finally to the teacher as Step 7 shows.

4. Algorithm Design

This sections discusses the major and minor algorithms that work together to generate the items. When "Algorithm Selection" function as shown fig.2 it is called, first item generated set G_j and temporary item set Q_j are initialized to empty; then it chooses proper major algorithm base on the cognitive type the teacher selected (at Line #2 to #9 show). .For instance if the algorithm receives apply cognitive type ct_A then it will invoke "Apply Item Generation" algorithm (as in Line # 4) passing c_t, ct as parameters.

ALGORITHM 1: Algorithm Selection
Input: set of cognitive type. $CT_j = \{ct_{j1}, ct_{j1}, ..., ct_{jn}\}$ and $ct \subset CT_j$
  c_t, concept node
Output: set of item generated $G_j = \{g_{j1}, g_{j2}, ..., g_{jn}\}$
Local : $Q_j = \{q_{j1}, q_{j2}, ... q_{jn}\}$, temporary set of item generated
1: $G_j \leftarrow \{\emptyset\}$, $Q_j \leftarrow \{\emptyset\}$
2 : case cognitive type (ct) of
3 :   Apply:
4 : $Q_j \leftarrow$ Apply item Generation (c_t, ct)
5 :   Analyze:
6 : $Q_j \leftarrow$ Analyze Item Generation (ct, ct)
7 :   Evaluate:
8:          $Q_j \leftarrow$ Evaluate Item Generation(ct, ct)
9: end Case
10: $G_j \leftarrow G_j \cup Q_j$

Fig. 2. Algorithm Selection Function

The "Apply Item Generation" shown in Fig.2 generates Apply cognitive items. When the algorithm is called the items generated variable G_j^A is first initialized to empty set (at Line # 1); then it retrieves Apply items rules R^A passing ct_A as parameter (at Line # 2). From (line # 3- #11) R^A is enumerated selecting rule attributes for item stimulus RA_x^S, stem RA_x^M and answer options RA_x^O respectively passing the current rule r_x.

ALGORITHM 2 : Apply Item Generation

Input : c_t, a concept node selected ; ct_A, an apply cognitive type

Output : G_j^A is subset of G_j, set of apply item generated

```
1 :   G_j^A ← { Ø }
2 :   R^A ← Retrieve Apply Item Rules by ct_A
3 :   for each item rule r_x in R^A
4 :       RA_x^S ← Select Rule Attributes for item stimulus ( r_x )
5 :       RA_x^M ← Select Rule Attributes for item stem (r_x)
6 :       RA_x^O ← Select Rule Attributes for item Answer Options (r_x)
7 :       s^A_x ← Stimulus Creation (c_t , r_x , RA_x^S)
8 :       m^A_x ← Stem Creation ( c_t , r_x , RA_x^M)
9 :       AO_x ← Answer Options Preparation (r_x, c_t ,RA_x^O)
10:      G_j^A ← G_j^A ∪ {s^A_x , m^A_x , AO_x }
11: end for
```

Fig. 3. Apply item generation algorithm

In Line # 7 "Stimulus Creation" algorithm is called passing concept node c_t selected, rule (r_x), and RA_x^S which then returns formatted item stimulus (s^A_x); Then "Stem Creation" algorithm is called with rule (r_x), which then returns formatted stem (m^A_x) (at Line # 8). At Line # 9, "Answer Options Preparation" algorithm is asked to prepare the answer options accepting r_x, c_t , RA_x^O as parameters and returns set of answer options AO_x . The stimulus, stem, and answer options created from Line # 7, # 8, # 9 respectively is used to create item {s^A_x , m^A_x , AO_x }and added to item generated set G_j^A. After all the iteration of the rules is completed i.e. from Line # 3 to # 11 the items as shown in table .1 will be generated.

ALGORITHM 5: Stimulus Creation

Input : c_t, concept node selected
   Item rule = $r_x \in R^A$.
   RA_x^S , set of apply item rule attributes for stimulus

Output : s^A_x , item stimulus created
Local : SV_j= { s_{vj1} , s_{vj2} , ... , s_{vjn}}

```
1: SV_j ← { Ø }
2: for each rule attribute r_xa in RA_x^S
3:     case r_ax^source of
4:        supporting:
5:           SP_j ← Retrieve random supporting attribute value pair passing  r_ax^name
6:           SV_j ← SV_j ∪ SP_j
7:        concept schema:
8:           CV_j ← Retrieve attribute value pair from concept schema passing c_t c_t , ra,r_xa
9:           SV_j ← SV_j ∪ CV_j
10:       concept node name:
```

Higher Cognitive Items Generation Algorithms

```
11:     cₙ ← Retrieve concept node name passing cₜ
12:     SVⱼ ← SV ∪ { rₐₓⁿᵃᵐᵉ , cₙ }
13:     end case
14:   end for
15:   TSᴬ ← Read stimulus template from item rule rₓ
16:   sᴬₓ ← Format stimulus template passing TSᴬ and SVⱼ
```

Fig. 4. Stimulus Creation algorithm

When the algorithm in Fig 4 "Stimulus Creation" is called with concept node selected c_t, element of stimulus rule $r_x \in R^A$, item rule attribute RA_x. First, the algorithm initialize stimulus attribute value pair variable SV_j to empty set (at Line #1): then loop through RA_x^S (from Line #2 - # 14) choosing the attribute source value r_{ax}^{source} of rule attribute object (.i.e. r_{xa}). For supporting (Line #4) it retrieves random supporting attribute value pair for the stimulus (SP_j) (at Line #5) and added to SV_j If the case is concept schema (Line #7) it retrieves attribute value pair CV_j (Line #8) and add it to SV_j (Line #9) from concept schema passing c_t if the case is concept node name (at Line # 10) the algorithm retrieves concept name with c_t then create { r_{ax}^{name} c_n }and add it to SV_j . Lastly, (at line #15). it reads the apply item stimulus template TS^A from the item rule r_x and format the stimulus template with SV_j (at Line # 16)

5. Evaluation Plan

The research team intends to invite secondary and undergraduate school to have hands on experience with Online Test System. The teachers will be given small task to (co-)create or their own knowledge maps or import from other teachers' creations. Then they need to associate the knowledge maps to one of their courses followed by generating items for different cognitive levels and creating test for their courses.

After teachers have used the system they will be given a questionnaire which has three parts. Part one is general information which collects their demographical information like gender, subject teaching and academic role. The second part has 43 5-point Likert scale questions [9] for gathering their perceptions toward the usability of the systems and the item generation feature. The third part consists of 40 items generated by the algorithms for higher and lower cognitive levels and the research team asks teachers to tell researchers which cognitive level each item may belong to. With the data collected, the research team can verify the usability of the system and the item generation feature; moreover, the accuracy and effectiveness of the item generation algorithms can be assessed.

6. Conclusion

Automatic item generation algorithms have been designed and developed for existing Online Test System research. The algorithms enhance the system with item generation feature and make it capable of generating items for both higher and lower cognitive levels. The details of the major and minor algorithms have been presented and explained. The research team would like to collaborate with teachers and schools to test the usability of the system as well as obtaining users perceptions and identify the cognitive level the items generated by the system belongs to.

References

[1] Alves, C. B., Gierl, M. J., & Hollis, L.: Using automated item generation to promote principled test design and development. In: the annual meeting of the American Educational Research Association. (2010) http://www.crame.ualberta.ca/files/AERA%202010%20Denver%20Task%20Model%20AIG.pdf
[2] Chang, M., Kuo, R., Chen, S., Liu, T., & Heh, J.: Developing True/False Test Sheet Generating System with Diagnosing Basic Cognitive Ability. In World Conference on Educational Media and Technology, pp. 5740-5748, Vienna, Austria, June 30-July 4, 2008. (2008)
[3] Chang, M., & Kuo, R.: Elementary Level Botanical Item Generation. Learning Technology. Newsletter, 11(3), 7-9 (2009)
[4] Gierl, M. J., & Lai, H.: Instructional Topics in Educational Measurement (ITEMS) Module: Using Automated Processes to Generate Test Items. Educational Measurement: Issues and Practice, 32(3), 36-50 (2013)
[5] Gierl, M. J., Lai, H., Hogan, J. B., & Matovinovic, D.: A Method for Generating Test Items that are aligned to the Common Core State Standards. Journal of Applied Testing Technology, 16(1), 1-18. (2015)
[6] Gütl, C., Lankmayr, K., Weinhofer, J., & Höfler, M.: Enhanced Automatic Question Creator – EAQC: Concept, Development and Evaluation of an Automatic Test Item Creation Tool to Foster Modern eEducation. The Electronic Journal of e-Learning, 9(1), 23-38. (2011)
[7] Hsu, C.-K., Chang, J.-C., Chang, M., Jehng, J.-C & Heh, J.-S.: An Approach for Automatic Learning and Inference by Knowledge Map. In the International Conference on Computers in Education (ICCE 2002), pp. 957-958, Auckland, New Zealand, December 3-6, 2002. (2002)
[8] Krathwohl, D. R.: A Revision of Bloom's Taxonomy: An Overview. Theory Into Practice, 41(4), 212-218. (2002)
[9] Likert, R.: A technique for the measurement of attitudes. Archives of Psychology, 22(140), 5-55. (1932)
[10] Schmeiser, C. B., & Welch, C. J.: Test development. In R. L. Brennan (Ed.), Educational measurement (4th Ed.) Westport, CT: Praeger Publishers. (2006).
[11] Stanescu, L., Spahiu, C. S., & Ion, A.: Question generation for learning evaluation. In the International Multi conference on Computer Science and Information Technology (IMCSIT 2008), pp. 509-513, Wisla, Poland, October 20-22, 2008. (2008)

Innovative Maker Movement Platform for K-12 Education as a Smart Learning Environment

Tapani Toivonen [1,*], Ilkka Jormanainen[1], Calkin Suero Montero[1], and Andrea Alessandrini[2]

[1] University of Eastern Finland, Joensuu, Finland
{firstname.lastname}@uef.fi
[2] Linnaeus University, Sweden
{firstname.lastname}@lnu.se

Abstract. The growth of the maker movement has created a demand to include tools for digital fabrication in the school curriculum to foster STEAM education. Yet, the tools used by the maker movement remain sparse and do not exist integrated in the same environment for educational purposes. In this paper, we introduce a smart learning environment that collects the tools of design, 3D-printing, programming, sharing and data analytics into the single frame where K-12 level students and their educators can *make* maker movement artefacts while enhancing their STEAM skills. Our developed smart learning environment gathers data from the users' digital trails and analyzes these data with several white-box data mining algorithms in order to support the educators' interventions in the *making* activities carried out in the classroom.

Keywords: Maker movement, Learning analytics, Educational data mining

1. Introduction

The maker movement emerged to empower people to appropriate technology creation [17]. It includes hobbyists, tinkerers, engineers and hackers who creatively design and built digital-age projects as a hobby and/or for profitable ends [17]. The roots of the maker movement lie outside of the formal school curriculum, however, lately there has been a growing interest to fuse maker movement activities with the K-12 education realm, in order to enhance the opportunities of STEAM education [1]. Among the *making* activities, designing, 3D printing, programming and eventually sharing the models of the created electronic artefacts can be highlighted [18].

eCraft2Learn is an ongoing H2020 two-year project that includes partners from several universities and digital fabrication companies [2]. The aim of eCraft2Learn is to enable K-12 level students and educators to be a part of digital-era maker movement through a craft- and project-based pedagogy, while learning different skills such as design, programming and 3D-printing. One of the ultimate outputs of eCraft2Learn is to develop a smart learning environment eCraft2Learn UUI (Unified User Interface) that would facilitate the access to several maker movement tools such as programming, 3D-modelling and printing, and designing and sharing tools through one single interface. A related output involves the development of an educational data mining application that analyzes users' digital trail data collected through eCraft2Learn UUI, to support the educator's understanding of the eCraft2Learn UUI context and to enable their smooth intervention in the learning process when needed.

This paper will provide an outline of the innovative smart learning environment platform eCraft2Learn UUI and its counterpart eCraft2Learn Educational Data Mining System (EDMS) that together combine the data analytics and the tools of the maker movement.

2. Background

The maker movement in K-12 education brings together multiple digital and physical tools and thrives on the "do-it-yourself" philosophy [17]. The most used tools include 3D-printers, Raspberry Pi computers, Arduinos and multiple actuators and sensors that can extend the functionality of the microcontrollers to the physical world [3]. Digital platforms for making also exists (e.g., Littlebits and GoJava). Yet, the maker movement platforms are still not usually counted as smart learning environments [4].

Smart learning environments include, for instance, adaptive learning systems and intelligent tutoring systems. But, the digital tools of the maker movement usually act as independent pieces of software and the students are required to use multiple instances of these different systems. Furthermore, smart learning environments usually collect data from the students who are using the system. This represents yet another challenge to the maker movement platforms and their relationship to the smart learning environments.

Therefore, the purpose of eCraft2Learn is to unify tools of brainstorming, design, 3d-printing, programming and sharing, key activities when *making,* into a single application interface, while the application itself collects data from the students' digital trails. The educators are then able to analyze the collected data using several data mining methods. Our approach aims at unifying maker movement tools with educational data mining tools to develop an innovative and smart learning environment for the maker movement and K-12 education.

Moreover, data mining processes usually operate in black-box models, where the data mining process is hidden from the users making the mining process and its results hard to interpret [5]. Following the do-it-yourself philosophy, we aim at implementing the educational data mining system for eCraft2Learn through *white-box* data mining models, where the mining process is visible and accessible to the user (i.e., the educators). The user is also able to modify and influence the data mining models that the system generates. This white-box approach to data mining applied to smart learning environments is innovative and transparent so that the data mining model itself explains the data mining results [6].

3. eCraft2Learn Unified User Interface

eCraft2Learn Unified User Interface (eCraft2Learn UUI) is a metro-based user interface [7], which collects the tools of the eCraft2Learn into one single frame. The prototype eCraft2Learn UUI is shown in Figure 1.

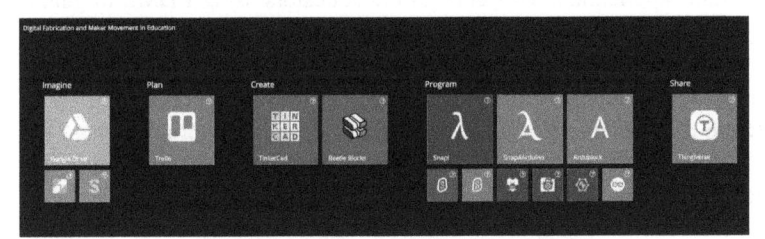

Fig 1. eCraft2Learn Unified User Interface

The tools of eCraft2Learn UUI can be divided into five categories: Imagine, Plan, Create, Program and Share. These five categories are the primary elements of the pedagogical approach behind eCraft2Learn and the students will concentrate on them while working towards the digital artefacts. Imagine category introduces the tools for brainstorming, ideating and initial designing of the upcoming artefact. Plan category takes the process to the concrete design after which the students are able Create models of the artefacts through the modelling software (Tinkercard [8], for instance). Program takes place in Snap4Arduino programming environment [9]. With Sharing, the users are able to share the developed making models and their designs to each other. In this way the eCraft2Learn UUI hosts tools for *making* in a single application. 3D printing in eCraft2Learn UUI works together with Ultimaker [10] 3D printers and the programmable microprocessors in eCraft2Learn UUI are Arduino microcontrollers [11].

eCraft2Learn UUI collects data from the student users by sending HTTP requests to eCraft2Learn Api whenever a user is interacting with eCraft2Learn UUI. Also, the tools hosted in the eCraft2Learn UUI collect data from the users, which is later analyzed in EDMS by the educators. For instance, in the case of Snap4Arduino the eCraft2Learn UUI tracks the user's code structure and the current state of the programming editor.

The entire eCraft2Learn UUI platform runs on Raspberry Pi 3s and is web-based. The only requirement of running eCraft2Learn UUI is to have Google Chrome browser installed. The tools that require, for instance, serial port communication

(Snap4Arduino) use Chrome extensions in order to access the computer's hardware.

4. eCraft2Learn Educational Data Mining System

Previous research (Jormanainen and Sutinen, 2014) [12] indicates that by opening the educational data mining process, the educators can deepen their understanding about the students' learning in the educational settings to enable interventions. Our aim when developing the educational data mining system for eCraft2Learn environment is to use a similar white-box approach to data mining and machine learning algorithms application. This enables the educators using EDMS to gain a deeper insight of the learning process of the students who are using the eCraft2Learn UUI in their maker projects.

EDMS uses various algorithms for evaluating student performace. The classifitation and the cluster analysis algorithms use white-box approach where the user can modify the algorithm models and get involved of the data mining process. The included data mining approaches of EDMS are ID3 decision tree classifier, Neural N-Tree neural network, multivariate normal distribution based outlier detector [15] and apriori [14] for association rule learning. Neural N-Tree is a cluster analysis algorithm that was developed for white-box cluster analysis processes.

ID3 is the most used type of decision tree algorithms [13]. ID3 decision tree is constructed by using a recursive top-down approach. In eCraft2Learn-EDMS, ID3 is trained with labels 'Well performed' and 'Not well performed' together with an initial training data set. The user of EDMS selects the data items from the dataset which are performing well and which are not. After the construction of ID3, the decision tree is rendered to the user and the final data is being classified in either well performing or not well performing datums.

The novelty of EDMS is that the user can change the rules of the constructed ID3 decision tree. If the user clicks the nodes of the rendered ID3, the user is able to change the pivot value, the operator or even the attribute that is being used by the node to divide the input vectors to the branches. Similar approach was used by Jormanainen and Sutinen, reporting that the teaching process benefits if the instructor is involved in the data mining process [12].

For the cluster analysis of EDMS, we developed a novel cluster analysis algorithm called Neural N-Tree. The aim of the new algorithm was to provide a white-box approach to the cluster analysis. The other requirement was that the algorithm would preserve the relationships found in the input vector space: some of the clusters are more similar to each others than other clusters.

Being a balanced binary tree, first Neural N-Tree is constructed recursively like any balanced binary tree. Each node is initialized with a random point vector with the lengths of the input space vectors. Afterwards the training set vectors are compared to the each terminal node of Neural N-Tree and the least matching unit (LMU) is chosen. The least matching unit is the terminal node with the least similar point vector compared to the current training set vector. The training set vector is then traversed from the LMU to the root by updating the point vectors of the sub-tree nodes with the formula

$$P(s + 1) = P(s) + f(\omega) * \alpha * (D(t) - P(s))$$

Where ω is the level function f: (1 / ((current level of the node in the sub-tree + 1) / (height of sub-tree + 1))), α is the learning rate of Neural N-Tree, P(s) is the current point vector of the node and D(t) is the current training set vector. The sub-trees are the level order arrays calculated from the current node of the traversal to the terminal nodes. After the first phase of the training, Neural N-Tree is trained from the root node to the terminal nodes by comparing the training set vector to the more similar child of the current node and by adjusting each sub-tree of the child node with the same formula as during the first training process. The comparison of the vectors is done through cosine similarity as it tends to reduce noise and performs well with high dimensional and sparse data [16]. That is, Neural N-Tree is actually a binary tree in the inner product space.

Neural N-Tree can then be used to cluster the dataset vectors by traversing the vectors from the root node to the terminal nodes (each terminal node is a cluster) by comparing the input vector to the points of the children of the current node. The training phase of Neural N-Tree (updating the sub-trees) enables the most similar clusters to be located under the same parent and the second most similar clusters to be located under the same parent of parent and so on. The white-box visualization of Neural N-Tree can then be rendered as it was an ordinary binary tree translated to the Euclidean space. Also, in EDMS user is able to change the point values of Neural N-Tree by clicking the nodes of the visualization and thus have an influence in the clustering process.

5. Conclusions and Future Work

eCraft2Learn UUI and EDMS form a novel smart learning environment that can be used to plan, design and create new maker movement artefacts as a part of K-12 STEAM education. EDMS uses a novel approach to analyze the data items by involving the educators in the process and letting the use to modify the data mining models in real time.

EDMS must be tested with the educators. Currently, EDMS contains many quite technical terms related to the data mining and machine learning. In the future, alternative terms must be considered to enable educators with no prior experience from data mining and machine learning to use EDMS.

EDMS development follows the findings of the previous research [12] where it was discovered that the white-box models in the context of educational data mining foster deeper understanding of the educational settings and learning process of the students for the educators.

References

[1] Martin, Lee. "The promise of the Maker Movement for education." Journal of Pre-College Engineering Education Research (J-PEER) 5.1 (2015): 4.
[2] eCraft2Learn web site. https://project.ecraft2learn.eu. Accessed 01-04-2018
[3] Schön, Sandra, Martin Ebner, and Swapna Kumar. "The Maker Movement. Implications of new digital gadgets, fabrication tools and spaces for creative learning and teaching." eLearning Papers 39 (2014): 14-25.
[4] Blikstein, Paulo, and Dennis Krannich. "The makers' movement and FabLabs in education: experiences, technologies, and research." Proceedings of the 12th international conference on interaction design and children. ACM, 2013.
[5] Cortez, Paulo, and Mark J. Embrechts. "Using sensitivity analysis and visualization techniques to open black box data mining models." Information Sciences 225 (2013): 1-17.
[6] Marquez-Vera, Carlos, Cristobal Romero, and Sebastián Ventura. "Predicting school failure using data mining." Educational Data Mining 2011. 2010.
[7] Kamimori, Shohei, Shinpei Ogata, and Kenji Kaijiri. "Automatic method of generating a Web prototype employing live interactive widget to validate functional usability requirements." Applied Computing and Information Technology/2nd International Conference on Computational Science and Intelligence (ACIT-CSI), 2015 3rd International Conference on. IEEE, 2015.
[8] Kelly, James Floyd. 3D Modeling and Printing with Tinkercad: Create and Print Your Own 3D Models. Que Publishing, 2014.
[9] Pina, Alfredo, and Iñaki Ciriza. "Primary Level Young Makers Programming & Making Electronics with Snap4Arduino." International Conference EduRobotics 2016. Springer, Cham, 2016.
[10] Ultimaker web-site. https://ultimaker.com. Accessed 09-19-2017.
[11] Arduino web-site. https://www.arduino.cc. Accessed 09-19-2017.
[12] Jormanainen, Ilkka, and Erkki Sutinen. "Role blending in a learning environment supports facilitation in a robotics class." Journal of Educational Technology & Society 17.1 (2014).
[13] Jin, Chen, Luo De-Lin, and Mu Fen-Xiang. "An improved ID3 decision tree algorithm." Computer Science & Education, 2009. ICCSE'09. 4th International Conference on. IEEE, 2009.
[14] Orlando, Salvatore, Paolo Palmerini, and Raffaele Perego. "Enhancing the apriori algorithm for frequent set counting." DaWaK. Vol. 1. 2001.
[15] Chandola, Varun, Arindam Banerjee, and Vipin Kumar. "Anomaly detection: A survey." ACM computing surveys (CSUR) 41.3 (2009): 15.
[16] Ertöz, Levent, Michael Steinbach, and Vipin Kumar. "Finding clusters of different sizes, shapes, and densities in noisy, high dimensional data." Proceedings of the 2003 SIAM International Conference on Data Mining. Society for Industrial and Applied Mathematics, 2003.
[17] Tanenbaum, Joshua G., Amanda M. Williams, Audrey Desjardins, and Karen Tanenbaum. "Democratizing technology: pleasure, utility and expressiveness in DIY and maker practice." In Proceedings of the SIGCHI Conference on Human Factors in Computing Systems, pp. 2603-2612. ACM, 2013.
[18] Martin, Lee. "The promise of the Maker Movement for education." Journal of Pre-College Engineering Education Research (J-PEER)5.1 (2015): 4.

Smart Interactions for the Quantified Self

Erik Isaksson[1,*], Björn Hedin[1]

[1] KTH Royal Institute of Technology, EECS school, Stockholm, Sweden
{erikis,bjornh}@kth.se

Abstract. The Quantified Self is a movement for collecting personal data with the goal of providing possibilities for new insights through reflecting on own relevant data, with applications in areas such as physical exercise, food, and health. When collecting personal data, difficulties may arise, such as information from different sources which cannot easily be combined, closed access to information sources, inflexible tooling for producing desired quantifications, varying precision of data used for producing quantifications, and a lack of control over data sharing for supporting relevant comparisons with others. In this paper, we introduce the concept of smart interactions, backed by linked data, as a means of introducing the QS through smart and personal learning environments, both for reducing the associated difficulties and further empowering the QS.

Keywords: Smart Learning Environments · Personal Learning Environments · Smart Interactions · Quantified Self · Linked Data

1 Introduction

The Quantified Self is a movement for people to log various personal activities and reflect upon these logs [1,2]. The tracked data varies greatly and involves everything from logging heart activities 250 times per second using advanced sensors to recording your morning mood with a suitable *emoji* every morning.

Both smart learning environments (SLEs) and personal learning environments (PLEs) involve the use of information brought in from multiple sources, whether they are sensors in the physical environment [3] or online services [4]. This implies a significant overlap with the concerns of the Quantified Self (QS), being "any individual engaged in the self-tracking of any kind of biological, physical, behavioral, or environmental information" [1].

However, in introducing the QS difficulties arise, involving, e.g., sometimes non-automatic data collection [1] and declining interest in visualizations over time [5]. The aim of this paper is to show how the QS could be brought into smart and personal learning environments, through a concept of *smart interactions* backed by linked data, and also how such interactions and learning environments could potentially reduce some of the difficulties of the QS.

The paper will first cover the relevant background, followed by a description of what *smart interactions* entail in the context of a PLE and how they may technically be realized through linked data. Finally, we exemplify through the chosen QS cases of food and energy, followed by our conclusion.

2 Background

It has been suggested that QS tools are suitable for reflective learning [2]. The reflection is often strictly personal involving only your own data, but in some cases includes comparisons with the quantifications of others. For example, most wearables for recording steps or sleep include comparisons with norm users. This is meant to lead to reflection on personal behavior and behavioral change, with benefits such as improved well-being and increased environmental sustainability.

The introduction of the QS into one's life can present major challenges. There might be multiple sources of data, either sources which are mostly automatic such as step counters or fully manual such as food logging. The data might need to be complemented with other data to be meaningful, e.g., data about the amount of energy used for heating a house is meaningful if you also have data about outdoor temperature, house area, and household size. Furthermore, interpreting data such as that for sleep can be difficult and experts could offer valuable assistance.

The Web is in part evolving into the Semantic Web, where not only documents but also data is interlinked, which is referred to as linked data [6]. URLs as locators for documents are generalized as URIs being identifiers for any kind of resource, which include things including "real-world objects and abstract concepts" [6].

In the same way that a URL affords access to a specific Web page and hyperlinks afford navigation between them, in linked data a URI affords access to information that includes links to related things for which information can also be retrieved. Linked data thereby offers a means for making data available on the Web in a standardized and interoperable manner. This makes it a suitable choice for open data, which includes data that governments or organizations have opened up with the purpose of enabling others to create innovative applications using the data.

Experience API (xAPI, previously referred to as the Tin Cap API) "is a specification for learning technology that allows recording a wide range of experiences that a user can have in different technologies or tools" [7]. Similarly to the approach taken in this paper, xAPI employs *triples* consisting of subject, predicate, and object. Generally, the subject is the learner, the predicate is the learner's action, and the object is the target of that action.

However, xAPI is designed primarily for the logging of learning experiences, e.g., with an aim of learning analytics [8]. *Smart interactions* in this paper are intended primarily for making more powerful interactions possible, while at the same time effectively offering the logging of learning experiences similarly to that of xAPI. This argument similarly also applies to the Activity Streams model [9].

3 Smart Interactions

Smart interaction in this paper partly refers to the instrumentation aspect of PLEs, which is that personally preferred services can be brought into PLEs through instrumentation [10]. Here, instruments are apps or widgets that, when placed in the Web-based environment, offer access to specific, external services. Widgets, sometimes referred to as gadgets [11], are apps that can be placed side-by-side in the environment, which thereby contains an adaptable set of instruments.

Smart interactions go beyond such instrumentation in three ways. First, the instrumentation is not necessarily that of an external service, which collects and manages the resulting data. Instead, what is being instrumented is the environment itself, and therefore the data resides there.

Second, from a developer's perspective, an instrument's utility lies not so much in the compliance with various application programming interfaces (APIs), but in offering affordances and models for the particular user interactions that take place in the environment on a semantic level, regardless of the form of the API.

Third, an instrument is not meant to be standalone and work in isolation, but to provide affordances for specific interactions, complementing other instruments. Thereby the combined functionality becomes "greater than the sum of its parts".

In the case of the QS, *smart interactions*, such as the logging of food intake and energy use, could be implemented as an interconnected set of widgets. The procedure of introducing QS into a PLE could thereby be as follows: (1) Find widgets for logging food intake and energy use and add them to the PLE. (2) Maintain a log of one's meals and activities involving energy use. (3) Find and add widgets for producing quantifications based on food intake and energy use and for sense-making and reflection. (4) Reflect on one's food intake and energy use.

As regards what is smart from the learner's perspective, there can be significant flexibility in how the respective widgets support effectively equivalent interactions. E.g., logging may be fully manual or fully automatic, with the possibility of the learner complementing or correcting what is logged. Moreover, the affordances of widgets can differ significantly depending on the needs and preferences of learners.

4 Realization

Smart interactions are carried out through a user interface, which is that of one of several widgets or apps. This may also involve interactions with the real world [12], e.g., through an app that also interfaces with the Internet of Things.

From a developer's point of view, an interaction such as logging that "I ate (a meal)" can be performed as shown in Fig. 1. It illustrates an HTTP *POST* request with content using the JSON-LD syntax [13] and a corresponding HTTP response. The request consists of a very minimal amount of information, which is intentional because it then also requires a minimal amount of effort on behalf of the learner as well as the developer. Further information can instead be added in subsequent interactions, possibly using other widgets or apps that may not necessarily be developed by the same person or organization.

```
Request:
POST /me/food:consume HTTP/1.1
Host: my.learningspace
Content-Type: application/ld+json
[...]
{ "@context": { "food": "http://purl.org/tellme/food/" },
  "@type": "food:Meal" }
Response:
HTTP/1.1 201 Created
Location: https://my.learningspace/me/j4w
```

Fig. 1. The interaction of logging that "I ate (a meal)"

The interaction in Fig. 1 is *"POSTed"* and thereby instantiated within my.learningspace. In accordance with linked data principles, the interaction is assigned a URI. Going beyond the basic principles, the request itself represents a *triple*, with the subject my.learningspace, the predicate food:consume, and the object a thing of the type food:Meal. Upon carrying out the request, the server indicates in its response which URI that it has assigned to the interaction. The triple will be offered in later retrievals of the information about my.learningspace.

If more information is to be added about an interaction, e.g., specifying the recipe of the meal, this could be achieved through a new interaction that links the prior one to other things, about which further information can be retrieved, e.g., in our case, a recipe along with details about the actual preparation of the meal.

5 Discussion

Quantifying the intake of food is one major area for the QS movement. There are several tools for recording the intake of food [14,15]. Such tools are typically used for health purposes, such as weight loss. It would be beneficial to be able to also use the same data for other purposes, such as, e.g., calculating the total carbon footprint of one's meals. However, it can be a challenge to access the data: even if an API is available, access through this API might not be granted on a general basis. Even when one does have access to the data, there is the question of being able to use it with a tool that matches the desired purpose, such as carbon footprint estimation. Challenges concerning data precision also need to be considered, especially when multiple information sources are combined. Logging one's every individual meal will be relatively precise, but for a family having a log based on supermarket receipts, there is a difficulty in associating amounts with individual family members. Moreover, a "tomato" can also result in different carbon footprints depending on factors such as how far it has been transported. More precise product groups or even product instances may be required for reasonably accurate quantifications.

Through the process of linking, both to external information sources such as estimated carbon footprints [16] and within one's own information space such as between purchases and meals, it should be possible to increase accuracy. While it is likely that a learner will not typically produce such links extensively, it could happen occasionally as part of a learning experience, e.g., when learning more about aspects of one's food intake. With technology such as machine learning and blockchains (e.g., for food provenance), such linking could become increasingly automatized, and turned into an implicit human-computer interaction.

Food involves use of energy. Moreover, we all make use of energy in other ways perhaps most directly in the form of electricity. Concerning electricity, access to data about home electricity use is increasingly available. However, challenges remain concerning the mixing of information sources as well as precision.

Another challenge is that of data sharing, e.g., in order to receive better advice on energy use and be able to make relevant energy use comparisons with other households. There is the question of whether to share the information directly, by offering access to a subset of one's PLE, or whether to share only relevant quantifications, such as, e.g., the average energy use per weekday.

Based on input from practitioners in the authors' project on energy advisory, there is also a need for data of a "static" or "soft" character, e.g., the number of people in the household and other specifics regarding the housing situation as well as personal motivations that influence what one is willing to change. While not strictly of a QS nature, such data concerns activities on a longer timescale. These activities involve interactions similar those of food intake and energy use, but are more dynamic in that they can be reconfigured by future interactions, e.g., driven by a newfound willingness to change something. By selectively sharing with friends, coaches, companies, and citizen scientists, such "static" and "soft" data interlinked with quantifications, new possibilities for insights through feedback can emerge based on comparing your own data with others.

6 Conclusion

Smart interactions based on linked data and the flexible instrumentation of PLEs offer both a framework for integrating various QS information activities, as well as a means for the dynamic introduction of QS into any learning environment.

In closing, generalizing the applications of *smart interactions* to areas beyond QS, it is possible to customize learning technology on a structurally deeper level. This will lead to different tools, possibly developed by different people and for different purposes, being able to *collaborate*—instead of merely co-existing—at the semantic level, and importantly, they can collaborate around the *same* data.

Acknowledgements. The research presented in this contribution has been partially carried out with financial support from the Swedish Energy Agency and the EC-funded projects ROLE (grant agr. 231396) and TELL ME (grant agr. 318329).

References

[1] Swan, M.: The quantified self: Fundamental disruption in big data science and biological discovery. Big Data 1.2, 85–99 (2013)
[2] Rivera-Pelayo, V., Zacharias, V., Müller, L., Braun, S.: Applying quantified self approaches to support reflective learning. In: Proceedings of the 2nd international conference on learning analytics and knowledge (pp. 111-114). ACM (2012)
[3] Koper, R.: Conditions for effective smart learning environments. Smart Learning Environments 2014 1:5. SpringerOpen (2014)
[4] Wilson, S.: Patterns of personal learning environments. Interactive learning environments. 2008 Apr 1, 16(1), 17–34 (2008)
[5] Prost, S., Mattheiss, E., & Tscheligi, M.: From Awareness to Empowerment: Using Design Fiction to Explore Paths Towards a Sustainable Energy Future. In: Proceedings of the 18th ACM Conference on Computer Supported Cooperative Work & Social Computing (pp. 1649–1658). New York, NY, USA. ACM (2015)
[6] Heath, T., Bizer, C.: Linked data: Evolving the web into a global data space. Synthesis lectures on the semantic web: theory and technology, 1(1), 1–136 (2011)
[7] Vázquez, M.M., Rodríguez, M.C., Nistal, M.L.: Development of a xAPI application profile for self-regulated learning requirements for capturing SRL related data. Global Engineering Education Conference (EDUCON). IEEE (2015)
[8] Bakharia, A., Kitto, K., Pardo, A., Gašević, D., & Dawson, S.: Recipe for success: lessons learnt from using xAPI within the connected learning analytics toolkit. In: Proceedings of the sixth international conference on learning analytics & knowledge (pp. 378-382). (2016)
[9] Snell, J.M., Prodromou, E.: Activity Streams 2.0. W3C Recommendation, https://www.w3.org/TR/2017/REC-activitystreams-core-20170523/ (2017)
[10] Isaksson, E., Naeve, A., Lefrère, P., & Wild, F.: Towards a Reference Architecture for Smart and Personal Learning Environments. In: Innovations in Smart Learning (pp. 79-88). Springer Singapore (2017)
[11] Google: Gadgets Specification, https://developers.google.com/gadgets/docs/spec (2008)
[12] Wiberg, M: Implicit interaction design. ACM Interactions blog, http://interactions.acm.org/blog/view/implicit-interaction-design (2014)
[13] Sporny, M., et al.: JSON-LD 1.0: A JSON-based Serialization for Linked Data. W3C Recommendation, https://json-ld.org/spec/REC/json-ld/20140116/ (2014)
[14] Lifesum, https://lifesum.com/
[15] MyFitnessPal, https://www.myfitnesspal.com/
[16] Hedin, B.: LCAFDB - A Crowdsourced Life Cycle Assessment Database for Food. In: 5th IFIP Conference on Sustainable Internet and ICT for Sustainability, Funchal, Portugal, 2017 December 6–7 (2017)

Smart watches for making EFL learning effective, healthy, and happy

Rustam Shadiev[1], Wu-Yuin Hwang[2], Narzikul Shadiev[3], Mirzaali Fayziev[3], Tzu-Yu Liu[4], Lingjie Shen[1]

[1]Nanjing Normal University, No. 122, Ninghai Road, Nanjing, China
[2]National Central University, No. 300, Jhongda Rd., Jhongli, Taiwan
[3]Samarkand State University, No. 15, University Boulevard, Samarkand, Uzbekistan
[4]Bei-Zheng Junior High School, No.14, Ln. 2, Sec.3, ZhiNan Rd., Taipei, Taiwan

Abstract. We designed learning activity in which language learning was combined with physical exercise. Our participants applied new knowledge to solve real life problems in their local community. Walking around the community during the learning activity enabled participants to be physically active. We provided students with smart watches to support their learning and monitor physical activities. We aimed to explore (1) whether our learning activity supported by smart watches can be useful for learning, make it healthy, and bring positive emotions to students.

Keywords: Smart watch, learning, physical exercise, authentic context.

1 Introduction

Learning in the class is abstract and disconnected from real-life scenarios because schools ignore the interdependence of context, situation and cognition [1]. Therefore, for learning to be meaningful and effective it should take place in authentic contexts [2, 3]. Students learn much better when they are immersed in real scenarios because their interaction with contexts has a profound impact on the way they interpret an activity [4]. More importantly, authentic contexts reflect the way the knowledge will be used in real life [5]. Such contexts can be found outside of school and they are meaningful, interesting, and related to students.

Students need to do physical activities regularly for maintaining their health condition. Benefits from physical activity on emotions and mood were reported elsewhere [6, 7]. However, still many people are not active enough and lead a relatively sedentary lifestyle [8]. To address this issue, opportunities to engage in physical activity should be increased. Teachers may organize learning activities that incorporate physical exercise; for language learning class, the instructor may assign students to solve real-life problems, e.g. to explain how to get to their home from school. Students may complete this task on their way from school to home when they walk instead of taking a bus and surrounding contexts will help students complete their assignments, e.g. make their route description more detailed and explicit. Such learning process will lead to healthy and happy learning.

Due to recent advancement in technological development, it became possible to produce smaller and cheaper computing devices [9]. Smart watches appeal to a broad range of user interests as it incorporates a wide variety of sensors for continuously measuring, recording and displaying different information, e.g. health-monitoring, location tracking, voice recognition, recording, and so on [10, 11]. This is why smart watches are regarded as potential tools to support both, learning and healthy living; particularly, if these two are combined into healthy and happy learning. Despite increased interest of research community in smart watches, not many studies have been carried out with such focus [12]. For example, the effectiveness of smart watches on healthy and happy learning has not been closely examined or affordances of smart watches for healthy and happy learning are still unclear. Furthermore, there is a little knowledge exists regarding student perceptions towards smart watches to support healthy and happy learning. This study aims to address this research gap.

2 Method

We designed English as a foreign language (EFL) learning activity in which language learning was combined with physical exercise. Eighteen junior high school students aged between 14-15 years old participated in our study. Nine of them were boys and nine were girls. They learned EFL in class via traditional instruction. After class, they worked on learning tasks outside of school by applying newly learned knowledge to solve real life problems using technology. Students worked on their assignments in their local community. Walking around the community to complete their assignments enabled them be physically active. It was assumed that learning in authentic environments combined with physical exercise will not only facilitate language learning but also make learning healthy, and bring positive emotions to students. We provided students with technology, such as smart watches (Figure 1-a), to support their EFL learning (Figure 1-b), to monitor physical activities (Figure 1-c), and to communicate with other students regarding their healthy learning (Figure 1-d). The aim of this study was to explore whether our learning activity supported by smart watches can be useful for EFL learning, make it healthy, and bring positive emotions to students. In addition, we explored student perceptions towards learning activity supported by smart watches and affordances of smart watches to support healthy learning. Finally, we studied how our research variables are correlated. To this end, the following research questions were addressed: (1) Do students perform better on a learning task when they use smart watches? (2) How students perceive learning activity supported by smart watches? (3) What are affordances of smart watches for healthy and happy learning? (4) How research variables of this study are correlated?

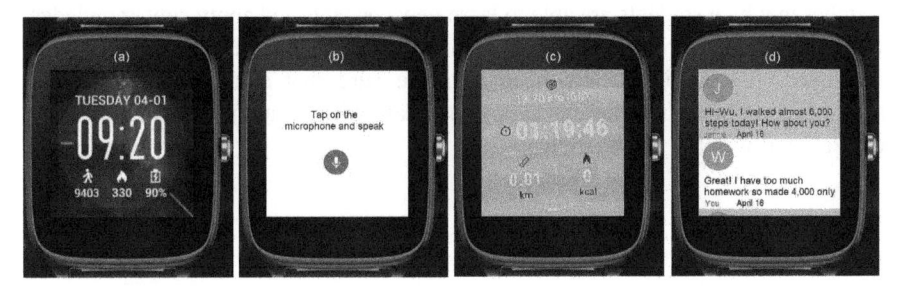

Fig. 1. Smart watch (a) for EFL learning (b), physical activity monitoring (c), and communication (d).

To answer the first research question, we carried out a pre-test, two mid-tests, and a post-test. With two mid-tests we assessed student learning performance on two tasks (i.e. one was completed with smart watches and the other without smart watches). We compared tests scores to investigate the effectiveness of our approach. For the second research question, we administered a questionnaire survey [13]. We also carried out interviews with all students to explore what affordances of smart watches for healthy and happy learning are. Finally, we carried out correlation analysis to test the relationship among our research variables.

3 Results and discussion

Students performed the best when they used smart watches for learning (t=2.149, p=0.046). Students perceived that smart watches were easy to use and useful for learning and learning activity was useful to be physically active and to have positive emotions. Students mentioned several features of smart watches which can facilitate EFL learning, physical activity, and positive emotions. For example, dictionary of smart watches helped students translate unfamiliar vocabulary (Figure 1-b) and fitness tracking tool tracked and recorded steps taken by students (Figure 1-c). Affordances of smart watches for healthy and happy learning were: hands free access, translation, speech-to-text and text-to-speech recognition, notifying, voice recording, information sharing, communication, fitness tracking, and happy learning. A significant correlation between learning performance and physical activity was revealed (r=0.652, p<0.05) suggesting that students who did physical exercise more were those who perform better. No correlation between learning performance and student perceptions was found suggesting that most students, no matter how well they performed, all had positive perceptions.

4 Conclusion

We make two suggestions: (1) to design learning activities supported by smart watches in which students are able to learn new concepts and apply new knowledge while physically exercise outdoors, so their happy and healthy EFL learning will be facilitated; (2) the instructors need to make sure that students are aware of affordances of smart watches for happy and healthy EFL learning, it will help them utilize smart watches more efficiently.

References

[1] Huang, Y.M., Shadiev, R., Sun, A., Hwang, W.Y., & Liu, T.Y. (2017). A Study of the Cognitive Diffusion Model: Facilitating Students' High Level Cognitive Processes with Authentic Support. Educational Technology Research & Development, 65(3), 505-531.
[2] Shadiev, R., Hwang, W.Y., & Huang, Y.M (2017). Review of research on mobile language learning in authentic environments. Computer Assisted Language Learning, 30 (3-4), 284-303.
[3] Shadiev, R., Huang, Y.M., Hwang, W.Y., & Liu, T.Y. (in press). Facilitating application of language skills in authentic environments with a mobile learning system. Journal of Computer Assisted Learning, DOI:10.1111/jcal.12212.
[4] Hwang, W.Y., Ma, Z.H., Shadiev, R.*, Shih, T.K., & Chen, S.Y. (2016). Evaluating listening and speaking skills in a mobile game-based learning environment with situational contexts. Computer Assisted Language Learning, 29(4), 639-657.
[5] Shadiev, R., Huang, Y.M., Hwang, W.Y., & Liu, T.Y. (2017). Cognitive Diffusion Model: Facilitating EFL Learning in an Authentic Environment. IEEE Transactions on Learning Technologies, 10(2), 168-181.
[6] Wankel, L. M., & Berger, B. G. (1990). The psychological and social benefits of sport and physical activity. Journal of leisure research, 22(2), 167.
[7] Biddle, S. J. (2000). Emotion, mood and physical activity. In S. J. H. Biddle, K. R. Fox; S. H. Boutcher (Eds.), Physical activity and psychological well-being, (63– 87). Routledge: London.
[8] Uher, I., Kuchelova, Z., Cimbolakova, I., & Pivovarnik, J. (2016). Physical activity and health. Prace Naukowe Akademii im. Jana Długosza w Częstochowie. Kultura Fizyczna, 15(3), 67-74.
[9] Kim, K. J., & Shin, D. H. (2015). An acceptance model for smart watches: implications for the adoption of future wearable technology. Internet Research, 25(4), 527-541.
[10] Bower, M. & Sturman, D. (2015). What are the educational affordances of wearable technologies? Computers & Education, 88, 343-353.
[11] Müller, L., Divitini, M., Mora, S., Rivera-Pelayo, V., & Stork, W. (2015). Context becomes content: Sensor data for computer-supported reflective learning. IEEE Transactions on Learning Technologies, 8(1), 111-123.
[12] Lungu, M.F. (2016). Bootstrapping an ubiquitous monitoring ecosystem for accelerating vocabulary acquisition. Proceedings of the 10th European Conference on Software Architecture Workshops. ACM New York, NY, USA.
[13] Hwang, W.Y., Chen, H.S.L., Shadiev, R., Huang, Y.M. & Chen, C.Y. (2014). Improving English as a foreign language writing in elementary schools using mobile devices in familiar situational contexts. Computer Assisted Language Learning, 27(5), 359-378.

StudentViz: A Tool for Visualizing Students' Collaborations in a Social Learning Environment

Alex Becheru, Andreea Calota, and Elvira Popescu

Computers and Information Technology Department, University of Craiova, Romania
becheru@gmail.com, popescu_elvira@software.ucv.ro

Abstract. Visualizations play an important role in learning analytics, supporting reflection and decision making. Network representations are commonly used for depicting social interactions between learners. While there are many network visualization platforms available, most of them are aimed at researchers, requiring social network analysis expertise. Our goal is to provide a simple tool for visualizing students' collaboration patterns in a social learning environment, which should be easy to use by the teacher. The paper presents a description of this tool (called StudentViz), some design and implementation details, and an illustration of its functionalities. It further shows that the tool adequately addresses the visualization needs of the instructors, fostering insight gaining.

Keywords: information visualization · visual analytics · learning analytics · graph plotting · social networks analysis · social learning environments

1 Introduction

Information visualization relies on the remarkable visual perception abilities of humans for pattern discovery [18]. It employs interactive visual representations in order to amplify cognition [12] and generate "insight" [5].

Visual approaches have been used in learning analytics, to help teachers and students explore learner traces from virtual learning environments. Various types of data can be included in a learning analytics dashboard, such as: *artifacts produced by learners, social interaction, resource use, time spent, test and self-assessment results*. The goal is to provide insight into learning data, supporting awareness and decision making, and increasing students' engagement and motivation [12].

In particular, social network analysis (SNA) and network visualizations have been used to investigate students' interactions taking place in educational environments [6, 16]. In this context, our goal is to visualize collaboration patterns between students in a social media-based learning space, which was less explored in the literature. More specifically, we are interested in studying learners' collaboration in our eMUSE social learning environment [15]. The platform integrates several social media tools (blog, wiki, microblogging tool) and provides value added services both for the students and the instructor (learner tracking, basic administrative services, data visualizations, peer assessment and grading support); more details about eMUSE can be found in [15].

We have already proposed a conceptual framework for knowledge extraction and visualization based on SNA in [2], which we have validated in [3]. *Gephi* network analysis tool [11] was used for all computations and graph visualizations, which adequately fitted researcher's needs; however, the tool was deemed too complex for instructors, who are not specialists in SNA or visualization. Therefore, we decided to build a simple network visualization tool, easy to use by the teachers and specifically designed to work in conjunction with our eMUSE social learning environment. The tool should provide useful and relevant visualizations from the instructor's point of view, therefore we first identified a list of visualization needs (VN) outlined by the teachers working with eMUSE:

- VN1. Visualize the general status of collaboration
- VN2. Visualize the status of collaboration for each community
- VN3. Visualize the status of collaboration for each learner.

Furthermore, the tool should support the processes of gaining insight through information visualizations, as identified in [18]:

- P1. *Provide Overview* - grasp the big picture of a dataset
- P2. *Adjust* - explore a dataset by changing the abstraction level or selection range (e.g., by filtering, grouping, aggregating)
- P3. *Detect Pattern* - find relationships, trends, or anomalies in the dataset
- P4. *Match Mental Model* - correlate the data with the user's mental model of it, in order to facilitate understanding.

Starting from these requirements, we designed and implemented our StudentViz tool, as described in the following sections. An overview of existing network visualization platforms is included in section 2. StudentViz functionalities and implementation details are presented in section 3. Its visualization capabilities are illustrated and validated in section 4. Finally, section 5 outlines some conclusions and future research directions.

2 Related Work

Networks or graphs are a common visualization method in educational settings [5]. They can be used to display information regarding students' interactions, which is particularly important in case of collaborative learning and social learning environments.

Many network visualization platforms (NVP) are available [7]; however, they are not specifically built for educational settings, so we wanted to investigate whether they can be used for our particular learning scenario, in conjunction with eMUSE platform. As our target users are instructors with limited technical expertise, we imposed some initial restrictions. The considered tools should be free, easy to install and use, and operating system independent. Moreover, they should provide high flexibility, so that instructors could adapt the visualization methods to their needs. Hence, our evaluation included the following platforms:

- *Cuttlefish*[1] is a very easy to use platform, but with limited capabilities and no flexibility; we also experienced some visualization glitches upon using the zooming functionality.
- *Cytoscape* [17] is an open source platform developed for molecular networks visualization, that has expanded its use across various network related research fields. Its standard features are relatively easy to use. However, the platform lacks flexibility of the visualization methods.
- *Visione*[2] has similar capabilities with *Cytoscape*, but it provides even less flexibility and the user interface is cluttered and non-intuitive.
- *Tulip* [1] is a visualization platform for relational data. It provides highly flexible visualization and a wide range of analysis capabilities for various research fields.
- *Gephi* [11] aims to be a general platform of analysis and visualization for all kinds of networks. Its clear design and resemblance with *Photoshop* make it very easy to use. Furthermore, its visualization capabilities are flexible and extensible through plugins.

Overall, we found *Gephi* and *Tulip* to be equally capable in terms of visualization functionalities; however, *Gephi* provided a better user experience, hence we chose to use it in [3].

Nevertheless, all platforms were considered too complex by the instructors, including many irrelevant functionalities for their purpose and requiring SNA expertise. Also, some of the desired visualizations (e.g., team and community perspectives) required significant effort in order to be generated with the existing NVP, starting from our available eMUSE dataset. Therefore, we decided to build a network visualization tool dedicated for the teachers, with a simple and intuitive interface, as described next.

3   StudentViz Tool Description

StudentViz is a data visualization tool purposely built to work in conjunction with our eMUSE social learning environment. Its aim is to provide suggestive visualizations of students' collaboration patterns, as they are recorded by the platform. More specifically, eMUSE integrates several social media tools that students use for communication and collaboration support. All students' social media traces are monitored and stored by eMUSE, and StudentViz uses these data

---

[1] http://cuttlefish.sourceforge.net
[2] http://www.visone.info/html/about.html

to draw the graphs depicting social media interactions between the students. A schematic representation of the data flow is shown in Fig. 1.

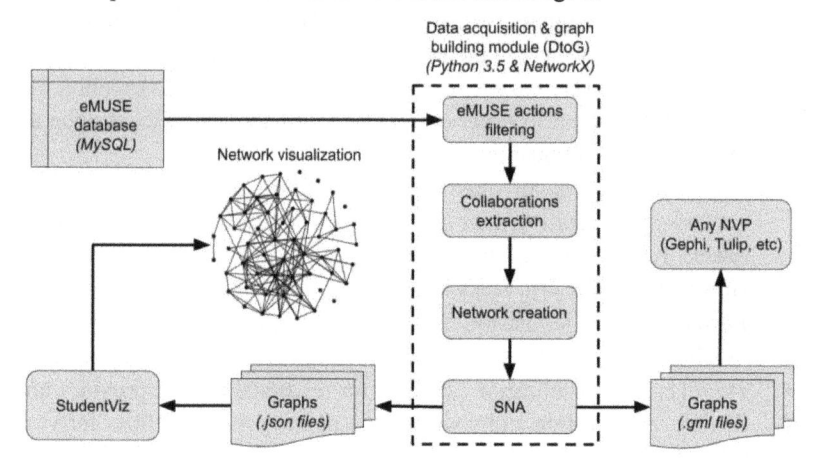

Fig. 1. StudentViz - network visualization data flow

The first step was to map students' collaborations as social networks. A *data acquisition & graph building* module (denoted *DtoG*) was designed to bridge the gap between the data source (eMUSE) and the visualization tool (StudentViz). DtoG processes the raw data collected by eMUSE, filtering the collaboration actions, and then creates various social graphs on which several SNA methods are applied. More specifically, directed graphs are built starting from students' interactions on the blog and microblogging tool; nodes represent learners and links represent messages exchanged through the social media tools integrated in eMUSE. The types of interactions (collaborations) taken into account on Blogger and Twitter respectively are detailed in [3]. These graphs can be exported in various formats (e.g., *.gml* or *.json* files), which can be subsequently input into any NVP, including StudentViz. As far as implementation is concerned, DtoG was built using Python 3.5 programming language and *NetworkX* graph analysis library [10].

In an attempt to reduce instructors' effort in using StudentViz, we decided to conceive it as a web application, thus eliminating the need of installation, configuration and manual updates. PHP, HTML5, CSS and *Cytoscape* JavaScript library were used for implementing the tool.

We also discussed with the instructors in order to agree on a set of graph plotting conventions that would be most suitable for their needs. Indeed, as mentioned in the Introduction, visualization methods should be easily correlated with humans' mental map (insight gaining process P4 [18]), thus reducing the comprehension effort. Therefore, we used directed graphs, in which nodes represent learners and links represent messages sent between the learners (on blog or Twitter). In order to expand the dimensionality of the information rendered in the graph, we introduced a color schema and magnitude schema for each graph element. Nodes shall be colored according to their affiliation to a certain community, i.e., nodes representing learners of the same team / community shall have the same color. In addition, links shall be colored according to their source node, in order to represent link direction. For example, if student A (red-colored node) sent a message to student B (green-colored node), then the link between nodes A and B shall be colored in red. The magnitude of each node (i.e., diameter) shall be directly proportional to a chosen SNA ranking: the larger the node, the higher the ranking. Thus, instructors can easily compare students according to a selected SNA ranking method, e.g., *PageRank* [14]. Furthermore, the thickness of each link shall be directly proportional to the strength / intensity of the collaboration between the two students; this can be computed through various methods, the simplest being the number of exchanged messages. Finally, nodes shall be labeled with a unique learner ID, in order to map the node to a particular learner.

We also decided to use force directed methods (FDM) for graph plotting [9], which generally produce aesthetically pleasing results. These methods are based on attractive and repulsive forces inspired from physics. Such forces attract nodes with high connectivity and repulse those with low connectivity, making the observation of communities of collaboration very intuitive. Moreover, the distance among nodes is inversely correlated with the strength of their influence on each other. Another advantage of FDM is their adaptability to various network traits, so they can be optimized from case to case.

Finally, StudentViz interface was designed in a simple and intuitive way. Two views are available, similar to *Gephi*: the *Main view* and the *Data view*. The *Main view* is further divided into 3 areas: *Options* area (left side), *Plotting canvas* area (center) and *Additional information* area (right side). Figure 2 provides a screenshot of StudentViz *Main view*. The *Data view* consists of a sortable grid of learners' attributes, including various SNA metrics. Similar views can also be found in *Gephi, Cytoscape* or *Tulip* under various names (e.g., *Data laboratory* in *Gephi*).

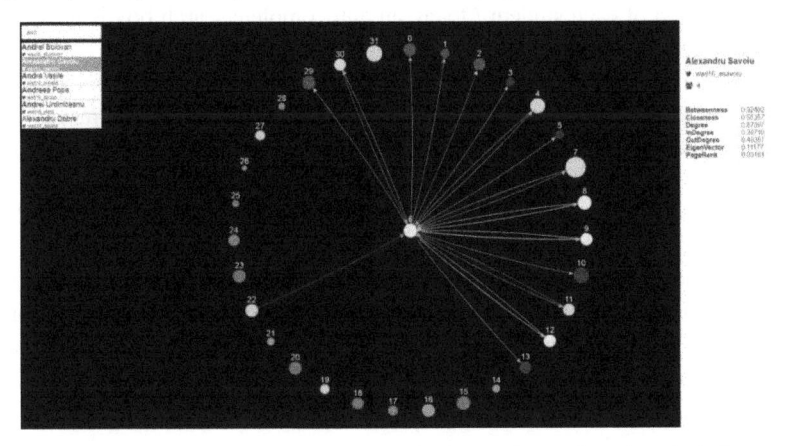

Fig. 2. StudentViz *Main view - Focus-circular* layout is employed; nodes' diameters are proportional to their *PageRank*, while their colors depict affiliation to a specific team

In what follows we present the *Main view* in more detail. The *Options* area allows instructors to interact with the visualizations and adjust them through various settings. Thus, as collaboration cannot be quantified by just one SNA metric, the teacher has the possibility to choose from several metrics: *betweenness, closeness, degree, in-degree, out-degree, Eigenvector* and *PageRank*. Through *betweenness* an instructor can determine the students that bridge community silos, those that facilitate the exchange of knowledge between communities. Students with high *closeness* values are positioned on various communication paths, playing an important role in knowledge diffusion. *Degree, in-degree* and *out-degree* centrality metrics can be used to determine the most / least active learners. Both *Eigenvector* and *PageRank* are measures of nodes importance that take into consideration qualitative and quantitative aspects; an important student is defined as one that has multiple collaborations with other important students. Additional information about these centrality metrics can be found in [4].

Another functionality provided in the *Options* area allows the instructor to select the graph plotting algorithm; available choices are: *WebCola*[3], *Cose-Bilkent* [8], *circular* and *focus-circular*, which will be discussed in the next section. Furthermore, the instructor can also choose the focus of the visualization: individual learners, teams or communities. This functionality is achieved by applying a *reduction transformation* on graphs that include all students; learners of the same team are represented as one node, while filtering out intra-team collaborations. Furthermore, the nodes' color can depict team or community affiliation; teams are predetermined from the beginning of the semester, while communities are non-formal and self-regulated. Community detection is computed using a Laplacian method [13].

An additional option available to the instructor is to load various graphs created by the DtoG module (e.g., graph containing all social media interactions among students, graph containing only collaborations on the blog / Twitter). Finally, for easy identification of each student / team, an autocomplete search box is provided, in addition to the full list of students.

The center area of the *Main view* consists of a black canvas on which the graph is plotted. The canvas color was chosen in order to provide a high contrast for the graph nodes and edges. The instructor can reposition nodes through drag-and-drop functionality; he can also select one node for detailed inspection, which sets the graph plotting algorithm to *focus-circular* and opens the *Additional information* area.

Finally, the right side area of the *Main view* provides information regarding the specific node selected: student name, team, SNA metrics values. This area is only displayed upon selection of a node, otherwise it is hidden, to allocate a larger space for the plotting canvas.

---

[3] http://marvl.infotech.monash.edu/webcola

4 Illustrating Visualization Functionalities in StudentViz

In what follows we show how StudentViz answers instructors' visualization needs, as they were specified in the Introduction (VN1 - VN3). It also provides support for the general processes through which people gain insight when using an information visualization system (P1 - P4) [18].

The context of use is a course on Web Applications Design, taught to 4th year undergraduate students from the University of Craiova, Romania, during 2016-2017 winter semester. 32 students used eMUSE platform (and the associated social media tools) for communication and collaboration support, in a project-based learning (PBL) scenario. Students worked in teams of 4 peers in order to develop a relatively complex web application. Based on the social media traces collected by eMUSE, a total of 2224 collaboration links were extracted (263 having distinct source-target pairs). Therefore, a social graph with 32 vertices and 263 links was built. More details regarding the PBL scenario and the process of extracting the collaboration links from blog and Twitter can be found in [3]. That paper also provides various graphs rendered by *Gephi* tool, which required specific SNA expertise to produce; here we present the graphs rendered by our StudentViz tool, which can be easily used by the instructor with no specialist knowledge.

Thus, Fig. 3 and 4 provide a birds-eye view on learners' collaboration, by using *Cose-Bilkent* and *WebCola* FDM respectively. These algorithms have low computational workload in case of small graphs and are suited for interactive applications, as they avoid the overlapping of nodes. As seen in Fig. 3 and 4, the general pattern of collaboration can be easily spotted, thus supporting VN1 and P1. High and low density areas of collaboration can be easily identified in both figures. Learners in the high density area (with nodes tightly plotted together) are significantly involved in collaboration with members of diverse teams; students in low density areas are those that teachers should focus on in order to enhance collaboration.

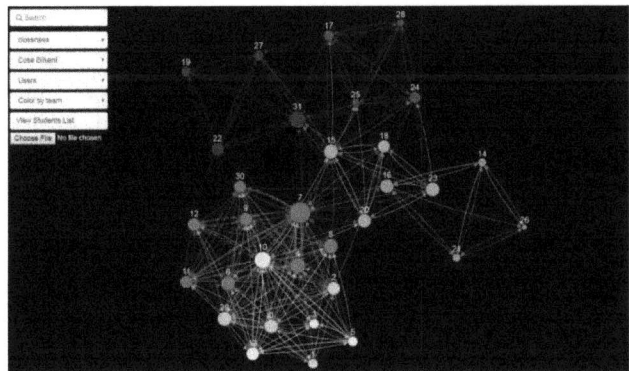

Fig. 3. Visualization provided by StudentViz using *Cose-Bilkent* plotting method. Nodes' diameters are proportional to *PageRank* metric, while their colors depict affiliation to a specific team.

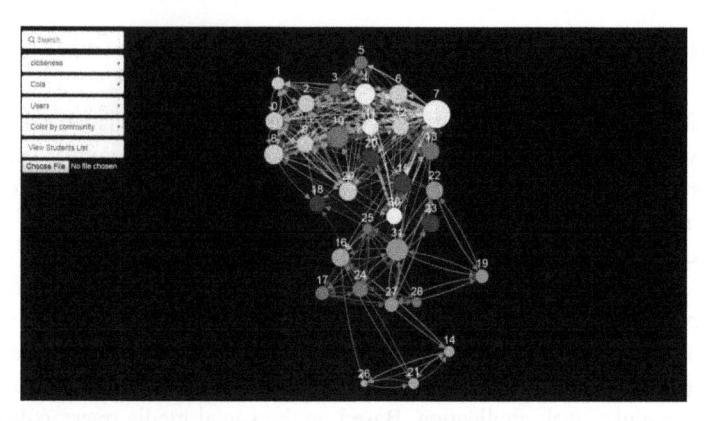

Fig. 4. Visualization provided by StudentViz using *WebCola* layout. Nodes' diameters are proportional to *PageRank* metric, while their colors depict affiliation to a specific community.

Although both algorithms produce similar visualizations, there are some variations that justify their complementary use. *WebCola* favors the identification of large communities of collaboration, as nodes are plotted in close proximity. However, this creates clutter, making smaller communities (teams) hard to spot. In turn, *Cose-Bilkent* favors the observation of smaller communities over large ones. Hence, *WebCola* and *Cose-Bilkent* also support VN2. In addition, these methods allow the discovery of the general structure and trends of collaboration, thus addressing P3.

Furthermore, instructors can better assess the collaboration between the teams by visualizing teams as nodes, like in Fig. 5 (which was obtained by applying the graph *reduction transformation*). Both Fig. 2 and Fig. 5 are illustrations of the *Focus-circular* plotting method, devised to clearly observe the status of a particular node (learner or team, respectively). The node of interest is positioned in the center of a circle on which the other nodes are plotted. Moreover, only the collaborations that involve the node of interest are rendered, to reduce unnecessary clutter and allow the instructor to focus on the particular node. Hence, these focus-circular visualizations address both VN2 (when nodes represent teams) and VN3 (when nodes represent students). Furthermore, P2 is also supported, as instructors can change the perspective on the dataset by selecting the node of interest.

Finally, the *Circular* plotting method, inspired by *Gephi's* circular layout, was devised to better observe the status of each team, as illustrated in Fig. 6. First, an average value of the selected SNA metric is computed for each team. The team with the highest ranking is plotted first, followed by the other teams according to their average metric rank, in a clockwise descending order. Individual nodes are also rendered in a clockwise descending order in the designated plot area for their team, according to their SNA metric value. Hence, the first plotted node depicts the learner with the highest selected metric value from the highest ranking team. This visualization method allows the teacher to observe the status of each team in comparison with other teams, but also the status of each learner in comparison with his fellow team members. Thus, both VN2 and VN3 are addressed by this visualization method; moreover, P3 is supported here, as instructors can discover collaboration patterns among teams and students.

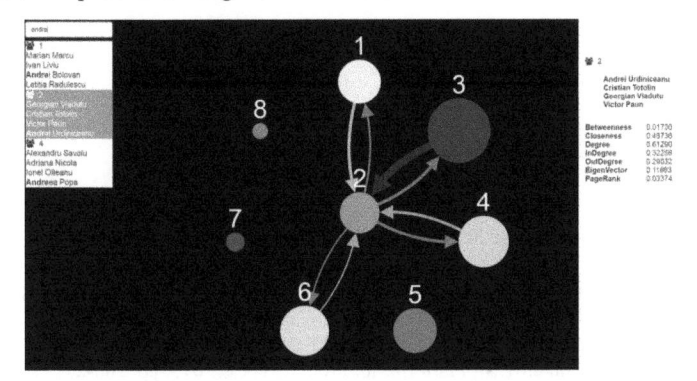

Fig. 5. Visualization provided by StudentViz using *Focus-circular* layout. Nodes represent teams and their diameters are proportional to *PageRank* metric.

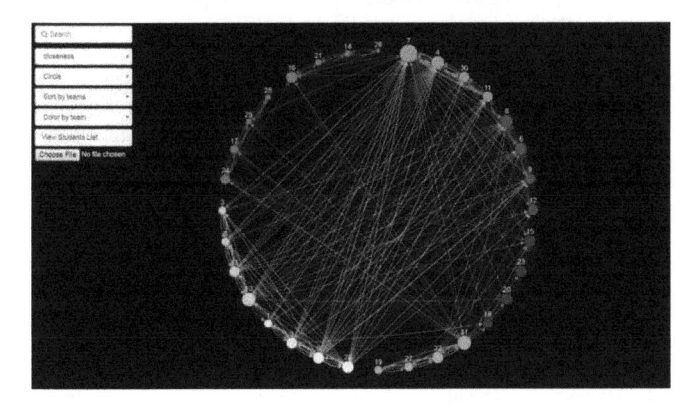

Fig. 6. Visualization provided by StudentViz using *Circular* layout. Nodes' diameters are proportional to *PageRank* metric, while their colors depict affiliation to a specific team.

5 Conclusions

Overall, with StudentViz an instructor is able to observe the collaboration status on different levels of network granularity, to emphasize different traits of the collaboration spectrum through various SNA metrics, and to turn their focus towards specific learners / teams. Hence, we consider that all basic visualization needs are successfully addressed, and an adequate support for gaining valuable insight is provided.

As future work, we plan to extend the tool with more visualizations, such as three-dimensional plotting methods and time-based representations. StudentViz could also be used to explore data from other social learning environments; the DtoG module is flexible and could easily be extended to accommodate different data sources.

References

[1] Auber, D.: Tulip - A Huge Graph Visualization Framework. In: Graph Drawing Software, Mathematics and Visualization, Springer, pp. 105-126 (2004)
[2] Becheru, A., Popescu, E.: Design of a Conceptual Knowledge Extraction Framework for a Social Learning Environment Based on Social Network Analysis Methods. In: Proc. ICCC 2017, pp. 177-182 (2017)
[3] Becheru, A., Popescu, E.: Using Social Network Analysis to Investigate Students' Collaboration Patterns in eMUSE Platform. In: Proc. ICSTCC 2017, pp. 266-271 (2017)
[4] Boldi, P., Vigna, S., Axioms for Centrality. Internet Mathematics 10(3-4), 222-262 (2014)
[5] Bull, S., Duncan, A., Ginon, B., Kickmeier-Rust, M.: Educational Data Visualisation Approaches and Open Learner Modelling. Project report, available at: http://css-kmi.tugraz.at/mkrwww/leas-box/downloads/D4.1.pdf (2015)
[6] Crespo, P.T., Antunes, C.: Predicting Teamwork Results from Social Network Analysis. Expert Systems 32(2), 312-325 (2015)
[7] Desale, D.: Top 30 Social Network Analysis and Visualization Tools. Available at: www.kdnuggets.com/2015/06/top-30-social-network-analysis-visualization-tools.html (2015)
[8] Dogrusoz, U., Giral, E., Cetintas, A., Civril, A., Demir, E.: A Layout Algorithm For Undirected Compound Graphs. Information Sciences 179(7), 980-994 (2009)
[9] Fruchterman, T. M., Reingold, E. M.: Graph Drawing by Force-Directed Placement. Software: Practice and Experience 21(11), 1129-1164 (1991)
[10] Hagberg, A., Schult, D., Swart, P.: Exploring Network Structure, Dynamics, and Function Using NetworkX. In: Proc. SciPy2008 (7th Python in Science Conference), pp. 11-15 (2008)
[11] Jacomy, M., Venturini, T., Heymann, S., Bastian, M.: ForceAtlas2, a Continuous Graph Layout Algorithm for Handy Network Visualization Designed for the Gephi Software. PLoS ONE 9(6), e98679 (2014)
[12] Klerkx, J., Verbert, K., Duval, E.: Learning Analytics Dashboards. In: Handbook of Learning Analytics, SOLAR, DOI: 10.18608/hla17, pp. 143-150 (2017)
[13] Lambiotte, R., Delvenne, J.C., Barahona, M.: Laplacian Dynamics and Multiscale Modular Structure in Networks. arXiv:0812.1770 (2008)
[14] Page, L., Brin, S., Motwani, R., Winograd, T.: The PageRank Citation Ranking: Bringing Order to the Web. Technical Report, Stanford InfoLab (1999)
[15] Popescu, E.: Providing Collaborative Learning Support with Social Media in an Integrated Environment. World Wide Web - Internet and Web Information Systems 17(2), 199-212 (2014)
[16] Romero, C., Ventura, S.: Educational Data Mining: A Review of the State-of-the-Art. IEEE Transactions on Systems, Man, and Cybernetics, Part C: Applications and Reviews 40(6), 601-618 (2010)
[17] Shannon, P., Markiel, A., Ozier, O., Baliga, N. S., Wang, J. T., Ramage, D., Amin, N., Schwikowski, B., Ideker, T.: Cytoscape: A Software Environment for Integrated Models of Biomolecular Interaction Networks. Genome Research 13, 2498-2504 (2003)
[18] Yi, J.S., Kang, Y.A., Stasko, J.T., Jacko, J.A.: Understanding and Characterizing Insights: How Do People Gain Insights Using Information Visualization?. In: Proc. BELIV'08, article no. 4, ACM (2008)

The *Edutainment* Platform: Interactive Storytelling Relying on Semantic Similarity

Irina Toma[1], Florentina Bacioiu[1], Mihai Dascalu[1,2], Stefan Trausan-Matu[1,2]

[1] University Politehnica of Bucharest, 313 Splaiul Independenţei, 060042, Bucharest, Romania
irina_toma@rocketmail.com, florentina.bacioiu@yahoo.com,
{mihai.dascalu, stefan.trausan}@cs.pub.ro
[2] Academy of Romanian Scientists, 54 Splaiul Independenţei, 050094, Bucharest, Romania

Abstract. Storytelling has been a part of human interaction since language emerged. It was initially used to convey information, describe events and people, and afterwards evolved into presenting examples of good and bad behaviors. However, stories are not limited to the early stages of child development as they can be used even in university lectures. The game described in this paper brings the power of storytelling in the learning environment, enabling teachers to present lessons as interactive stories. In the context of our serious game, students test their knowledge by answering with free text inputs to the questions presented by the virtual assistant in a challenging and entertaining environment. The prototype version was tested by a group of 26 students who found the game concept very interesting and provided valuable feedback in terms of user experience and functionality.

Keywords: Serious games · Digital storytelling · Semantic similarity · Text cohesion · Natural Language Processing

1 Introduction

Lectures are a central element of the learning and teaching process in traditional learning environments. Usually, teachers present a large amount of information which students cannot assimilate only by listening, therefore they take notes. Even though taking notes is recommended, students end up focusing on the writing task and fail to pay attention to the whole lesson or to the teacher's explanations. In order to make lectures more appealing to students, presentations can be transformed from monologues to dynamic lectures, during which students ask questions or expose their own knowledge. In this manner, learners make connections between previous knowledge and the new information, thus creating an easier and more productive learning process.

When the information to be learnt is completely new, students cannot relate on their previous knowledge, nor can they make new associations within their conceptual network [1]. One choice of learning is to memorize the concept, which has the disadvantage of being obliterated if the concept is not exercised enough [2]; a potential alternative is to present the information as a story. Storytelling is a frequently used method of communication encountered in the human society [3]. By introducing storytelling in the learning process, students increase their learning skills and can collaborate better [4].

The following sections describe the concept of storytelling and its transposition within our serious game – *Edutainment*. Section 2 describes the evolution of storytelling and the advantages of using it in the learning environment. Section 3 presents available storytelling games, while section 4 details our *Edutainment* Platform, a serious game designed for interactive lectures. The last two sections focus on results and conclusions.

2 Storytelling Evolution

Storytelling, as defined by Miller and Pennycuff [5], is the act of describing a narrative event to one or more listeners by using voice and gestures. Storytelling dates back to the emergence of human language, at least 50,000 years ago [6], and it was initially used in the context of hunting and gathering [7]. Also, without the means of written language, storytelling became the only way to transmit the culture, values and history of people, structured as verses, songs, short stories or tales of wisdom [8]. Later on, together with the development of the printing press, stories became widely available. In the beginning, stories were used as education material, to exemplify to children good and bad behaviors, or to inform about different historical events. Afterwards, stories' purpose switched to entertainment, without any intention to educate. However, storytelling can be used in multiple ways, either in the educational domain, or in the entertaining one. This paper focuses on the education area, in which storytelling is a powerful tool used by teachers to help students understand complex events. The proposed technique is an active learning strategy as it promotes engaging activities, collaborative learning and a problem-based learning environment [9, 10].

Alongside with the emergence and availability of new technologies, over the past ten years, teachers have been introducing multimedia productions in the learning environment, therefore upgrading the original storytelling technique to *digital storytelling* [11]. This new technique involves the usage of computer-based graphics, computer-generated texts, videos, pictures, and music [12] in order to create engaging and entertaining environments for learning purposes. Digital stories are separated into three main categories based on the type of provided content [13]:

- *Personal narratives*. This is the most popular type of digital stories in which authors describe their personal experiences. These stories can have an emotional impact on the receiver and can be meaningful to them.
- Stories that *inform or instruct*. This type of digital stories is used to teach various subjects and can be employed by teachers in the classroom.
- Stories that *present and examine historical events*. These stories are created by both teachers and students, and recall events from the past.

Digital storytelling impacts students from an early stage of the learning process, during language and vocabulary acquisition. Students benefit from listening to stories while developing listening and comprehension skills. Moreover, they pay attention to pronunciation and can deduce the meaning of unknown words from the context [14]. When recording their own digital stories, students develop their critical thinking, analytical, persuasive, technological, and artistic skills [15]. Creating a digital story consists of two phases. In the first phase, students gather information from the Internet, filter it and rephrase it to better appeal to the target audience. The second phase is represented by the visual representation of the gathered materials. Students use different programs to process videos, images and add text, therefore improving their computer and artistic skills.

3   Storytelling Games

Current educational curricula have evolved from using plain books to interactive ones that employ digital images, videos, and storytelling. One potential further step in the development consists of the inclusion of storytelling into serious games. Games currently available on the market present to users a method of sharing their own stories, listening to others or interacting with stories based on predefined paths. However, these games do not let users input free text, nor interact with the story. Three serious games already available on the market are described below.

SAGE (Storytelling Agent Generation Environment) [16] is a storytelling game that has two interaction models. The first one is storytelling, where children share a story from their lives, a virtual character listens to it, and responds with a traditional tale. The second interaction mode consists of creating a story to be shared with other children. The story is created using a visual authoring language that allows children to program the interactions and conversational flow between the listener and the storyteller, as well as the movement of the interactive stuffed animal.

oTTomer [17] presents a story for young children that takes place on a distant planet bearing the same name. oTTomer is a peaceful place to live until it is invaded by mutants, called the Odoracs. The story is structured in several episodes, in which children face different situations, and their reactions change the outcome of the story. The goal of the game is to catch the Odoracs and make them leave the planet.

Lifeline   (https://www.bigfishgames.com/daily/3mingames/lifeline/)   is   an interactive fiction game for mobile devices in which players must make decisions to help Taylor, the protagonist, after crash landing on the moon of an alien planet. The game can be played in real world time, as users receive notifications from Taylor asking what he should do next. The user selects the next action from a list of possible actions, thus driving the story to different endings.

4 The Edutainment Platform

The *Edutainment* Platform is a serious game based on text analysis, whose main goal is to support students to learn and test their knowledge in a challenging and entertaining environment. It is based on the concept of Lifeline, but brings educational value by allowing students to input free text. The introduced text is analyzed using *ReaderBench* [18, 19], a framework relying on advanced Natural Language Processing techniques.

The system has two modules, one for teachers and one for students. Within the teacher mode, users can add, edit, delete, and view existing lessons, whereas in the student module, users learn by playing the lesson. The two modules have a common starting point, the authentication page, where users login with their account or create a new one. A detailed presentation of each module is presented in the subsequent sections.

4.1 Overview of the *ReaderBench* Platform

ReaderBench [20, 21] is a framework for advanced Natural Language Processing that focuses on text cohesion. The *Edutainment* Platform uses two web services that *ReaderBench* provides, namely the text similarity endpoint and the similar concepts endpoint.

The text similarity endpoint computes the similarity score between two texts. It takes as input: a) the two texts being processed, b) the processing language (e.g., English or French), c) the semantic model used for computation (Latent Semantic analysis – LSA [22], Latent Dirichlet Allocation - LDA [23], or word2vec [24]) and 4) the corresponding corpus used for training the semantic model (e.g., TASA for English or "Le Monde" for French- http://lsa.colorado.edu/spaces.html). In our particular case, the *Edutainment* Platform is available only for the English language, it uses LSA as semantic model and TASA as corpus for building word vectors. The output of the endpoint is a value between 0 and 1, corresponding to a normalized cosine similarity score between the texts.

The similar concepts endpoint outputs a list of inferred, semantically related, concepts and their similarity score, based on an input word. The endpoint is used in a similar manner to the text similarity endpoint, noting that it takes as input one word instead of two texts.

4.2 Teacher Module

The teacher module contains administrative functionalities such as adding lessons, editing, deleting, as well as viewing an already existing lesson. The most important functionality in the teacher module is the *Add Lesson* action (see Fig. 1). All the fields available in this page must be filled in by the teacher: a) the title of the lesson, b) its description, as well as c) a set of 10 questions, each with three possible answers and value points. The number of answers corresponds to three knowledge levels: good, medium, and poor. Each answer is assigned value points based on accuracy and completeness in order to emphasize the knowledge level within the obtained score.

Each answer added by the teacher is checked against the initial question. The application uses the text similarity endpoint from *ReaderBench* to compute the similarity score between the question and the current answer. If the score is lower than an imposed threshold (manually set at .3), the system displays a warning message in the UI, asking the teacher to review the answer as it exhibits a low semantic similarity. Thereafter, the teacher can decide whether to change the answer or not; thus, the application assists users to add content in a coherent manner by ensuring a high similarity between questions and their corresponding answers. Moreover, in order to better engage students in the game, each question has a list of hidden keywords that, once used, add points to the student's score. The keywords are suggested automatically using the similar concepts endpoint provided by *ReaderBench*. Teachers can select these suggested concepts to be added in the keywords list. Due to the fact that our analysis is centered on texts, we opted not to include visual elements including images or videos in the interactive stories, but to focus only on branching scenarios that are based on textual inputs.

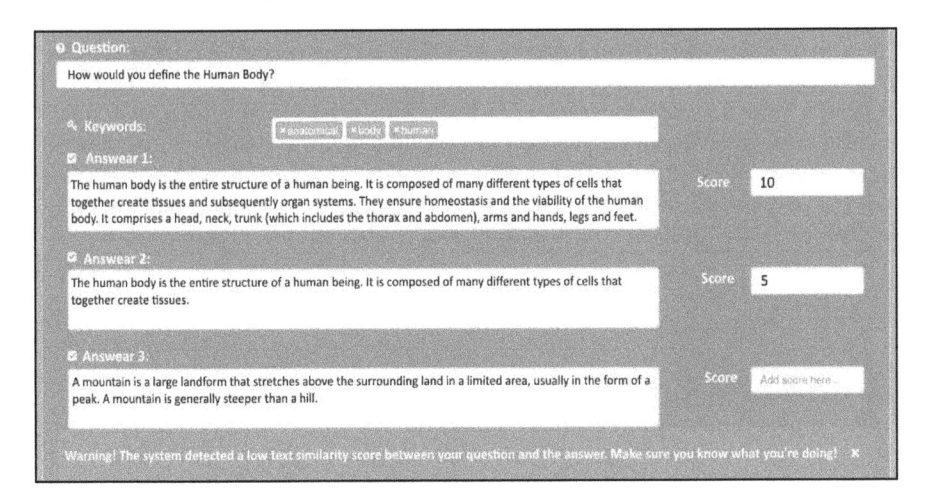

Fig. 1. *Edutainment* – Interface for adding a new lesson.

After adding the lesson questions, the lesson hierarchy represents the next step towards creating a functional lesson (see Fig. 2). The purpose of the hierarchy is to link answers to follow-up questions in order to generate multiple study paths.

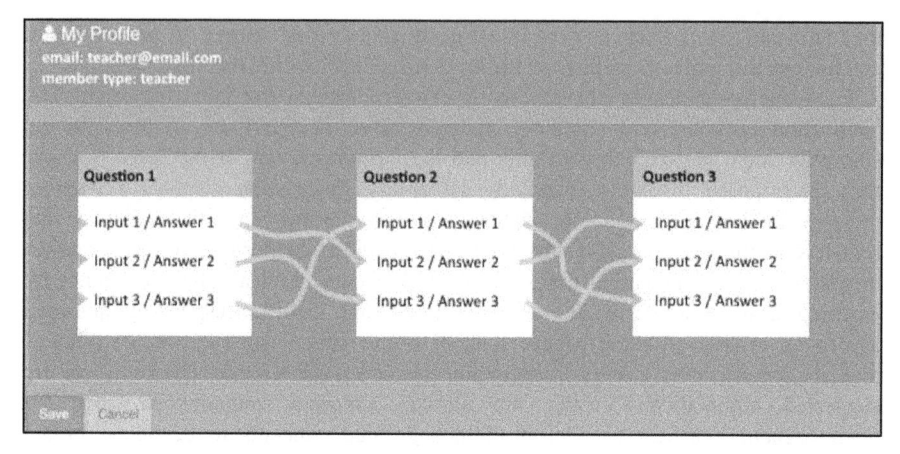

Fig. 2. *Edutainment* – Lesson hierarchy depicting connections between answers and questions.

4.3 Student Module

The active lessons added by the teacher are displayed to students after logging in the application (see Fig. 3). Each lesson has a "*Play*" button that takes the user to a dedicated "*Play Lesson*" page (see Fig. 4) that is structured as a chat window in which students answer the questions provided by the virtual assistant. The game starts when the user types "*START*" in the chat environment and the first displayed question is the root from the lesson hierarchy. The novelty of this game consists of the multiple paths students can follow, which are semantically mapped to teacher's potential answers.

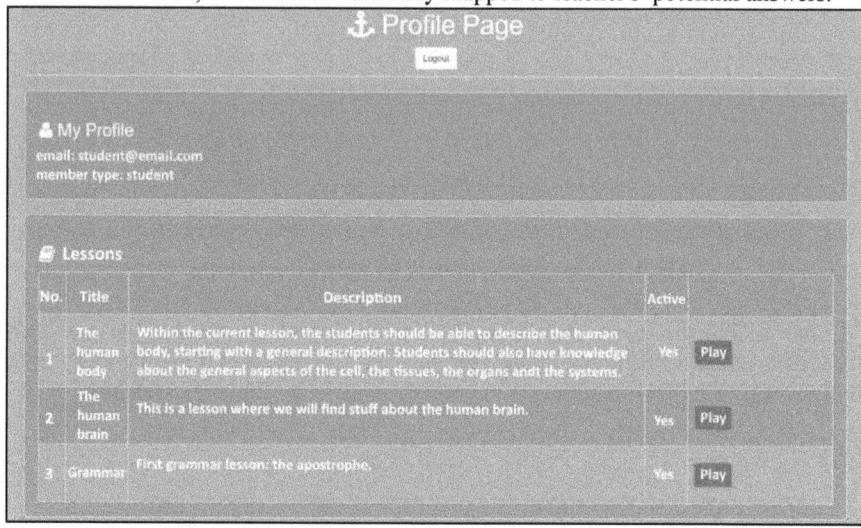

Fig. 3. *Edutainment* – Lessons available within the student module.

Users are entitled to one answer per question. Once the answer is introduced, it is sent to the *ReaderBench* text similarity endpoint together with each response defined by the teacher. After the similarity scores are computed, the student is awarded the number of points associated to the most similar predefined answer, while the next question in the hierarchy is displayed.

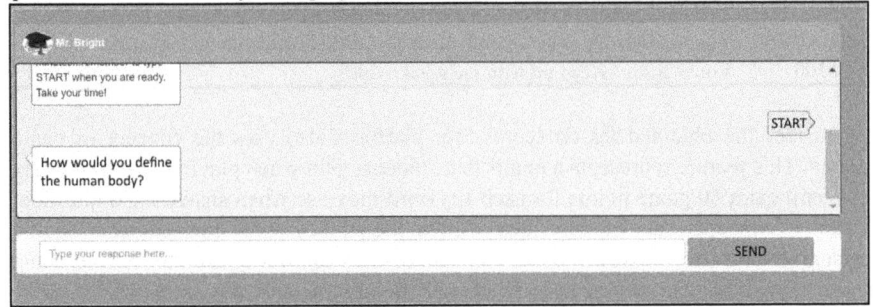

Fig 4. *Edutainment* – The flow for playing a lesson, i.e. an interactive story.

In order to make the chat more realistic, and to give users the illusion that the virtual character resembles a person, a delay of 2000ms is added before displaying the next question. If there is no question to be shown in the hierarchy, the lesson ends and feedback is displayed.

4.4 Lesson Feedback and Game Points

During each lesson, students receive points for their answers. The score is computed based on the value points added by the teacher for the response that best matched the student's answer and the similarity score between these two. The following formula is used to compute the score:

$$S = \left(\sum_{i=1}^{n} SSi * VP_i\right)/n \qquad (1)$$

where S is the final score, n is the overall number of questions, SS_i represents the similarity score between the student's response and the teacher's matching response for question i, and VP_i is the value points assigned by the teacher for a predefined answer from question i.

The maximum score for each lesson is limited to 10,000 points and can be achieved if players respond perfectly to all questions, and the similarity scores between their responses and the teacher's matching answer is always 1. This is the ideal case, highly unlikely to appear. Because of this, different score thresholds have been added, each corresponding to a feedback message presented in Table 1.

Table 1. Provided feedback based on obtained scores.

Final Score (Points)	Provided messages
< 4500	Don't worry, keep studying and you'll do better next time!
4500 - 6499	You have basic knowledge! Keep learning and you will do great next time!
6500 - 8499	Your knowledge is very good! Keep on working and you will shine next time!
>= 8500	You're a star! Keep up with the good work!

Besides the obtained lesson scores, our platform also uses the concept of game points. This feature represents a bonus that students gain when playing a lesson. Users can earn extra 50 game points for each keyword they use when answering a question. Usually, concepts can be described with a list of keywords that students should remember and use. However, users can successfully answer questions without using these keywords; hence, there is no need to artificially increase the score of a lesson by adding the game points to the total score. In the end, game points are only a method for rewarding students and keeping them engaged and motivated to play the game.

5   Results and Discussions

A group of 26 users, aged 21 to 35 years old, 38% females, 76% active in the IT domain, were asked to play on the *Edutainment* Platform: 17 on the student module and 9 on the teacher module. All users were asked to respond to surveys with ratings on a 5-point Likert Scale (1–completely disagree; 5–completely agree) and four free input questions, covering their perspective on the specific module.

In terms of reliability statistics, Intraclass Correlation Coefficients [25] and Cronbach's Alpha were computed for both the teacher and the student modules. The values, ICC - .395 for the Teacher module and .461 for the Student module, respectively Cronbach's Alpha .395 and .423, denote a low agreement between users, thus exhibiting different perceptions with regards to the game. On the teacher side, 4 out of 9 users appreciated the innovative idea of the game and the fact it can be applied in any domain, from storytelling to actual school lessons. From a functionality point of view, the lesson hierarchy was appealing to users, but the manner in which lessons are added created confusion among users. While relating to the free input questions, two users considered a limitation the fixed number of answers for each question. In terms of the UI, the interface received a good feedback from 50% of the users. People stated it is easy to use, friendly and intuitive and one user considered optimizing the interface for mobile users.

From a student module perspective, users agreed that the aim of the application is clear, but had divergent opinions on the application's ease of use; 50% of the users considered it should be improved in terms of design and user experience. Users suggested adding more interactive elements, such as animations, graphic feedback and a ranking system. In addition, 5 users felt the need to include a comprehensive feedback at the end of the game that contains insights on why their answers were incomplete or wrong.

6 Conclusions

The *Edutainment* Platform is a serious game designed to consider free input text interactions in digital storytelling. The stories have educational content and bring innovation because user's evolution considers different paths, depending on the provided answers. The free input text is analyzed using our *ReaderBench* framework and the user is directed onto different story paths based on the obtained semantic similarity scores. The system is composed of a teacher and a student module. Teachers are responsible for adding stories and configuring the lesson paths, while students follow these paths by interacting with the story.

The application is in an early stage of development and it has limitations in terms of provided features. Therefore, our prototype was tested only by a group of 26 users, which appreciated the concept of the game and about half of them found the interface intuitive and easy to use. Even though the values for the calculated reliability statistics denoted a low agreement among raters, feedback was drawn from the free input questions. Suggestions such as displaying more feedback to users, adding more interactive elements in the interface and providing more flexibility in terms of lesson creation, as well as hierarchies, will be considered for implementation in future releases. Moreover, subsequent evaluations will consider a wider audience, a refinement of the questions from the survey, as well as providing additional guidance to help learners understand the game concept and how to properly assess it.

Acknowledgements. This research was partially supported by the 644187 EC H2020 *Realising an Applied Gaming Eco-system* (RAGE) project and by the FP7 2008-212578 LTfLL project.

References

1. Wolter, B.: Lexical network structures and L2 vocabulary acquisition: The role of L1 lexical/conceptual knowledge. Applied Linguistics, 27(4), 741-747 (2006)
2. Thornbury, S.: How to teach vocabulary, Vol. 1. Pearson Education India, Longman Essex (2006)
3. Chung, S.-K.: Digital storytelling in integrated arts education. The International Journal of Arts Education, 4(1), 33-50 (2006)
4. Mello, R.: The Power of Storytelling: How Oral Narrative Influences Children's Relationships in Classrooms. International Journal of Education & the Arts, 2(1) (2001)
5. Miller, S., Pennycuff, L.: The power of story: Using storytelling to improve literacy learning. Journal of Cross-Disciplinary Perspectives in Education, 1(1), 36-43 (2008)
6. Wang, W.S., Minett, J.W.: The invasion of language: emergence, change and death. Trends in ecology & evolution, 20(5), 263-269 (2005)

7. Sugiyama, M.S.: Narrative theory and function: Why evolution matters. Philosophy and Literature, 25(2), 233-250 (2001)
8. Andrews, D.H., Hull, T.D., Donahue, J.A.: Storytelling as an instructional method: Definitions and research questions. Interdisciplinary Journal of Problem-based Learning, 3(2), 3 (2009)
9. Prince, M.: Does active learning work? A review of the research. Journal of engineering education, 93(3), 223-231 (2004)
10. Moitra, K.: Storytelling as an Active Learning Tool to Engage Students in a Genetics Classroom. Journal of microbiology & biology education, 15(2), 332 (2014)
11. Sadik, A.: Digital storytelling: A meaningful technology-integrated approach for engaged student learning. Educational technology research and development, 56(4), 487-506 (2008)
12. Robin, B.R.: Digital storytelling: A powerful technology tool for the 21st century classroom. Theory into practice, 47(3), 220-228 (2008)
13. Robin, B.: The educational uses of digital storytelling. Technology and teacher education annual, 1, 709 (2006)
14. Brown, R., Waring, R., Donkaewbua, S.: Incidental vocabulary acquisition from reading, reading-while-listening, and listening to stories. Reading in a foreign language, 20(2), 136 (2008)
15. Yuksel, P., Robin, B.R., McNeil, S.: Educational uses of digital storytelling around the world. In: Proceedings of Society for Information Technology & Teacher Education International Conference, Vol. 1, pp. 1264-1271 (2011)
16. Bers, M.U., Cassell, J.: Children as designers of interactive storytellers:"Let me tell you a story about myself...". Human cognition and social agent technology, 19, 61 (2000)
17. Valinho, P., Correia, N.: oTTomer: An interactive adventure system for children. In: Proceedings of the 1st ACM workshop on Story representation, mechanism and context, pp. 71-74. ACM (2004)
18. Dascalu, M., Dessus, P., Trausan-Matu, S., Bianco, M., Nardy, A.: ReaderBench, an environment for analyzing text complexity and reading strategies. In: 16th Int. Conf. on Artificial Intelligence in Education (AIED 2013), Vol. LNCS 7926, pp. 379–388. Springer, Memphis, USA (2013)
19. Dascalu, M., Stavarache, L.L., Dessus, P., Trausan-Matu, S., McNamara, D.S., Bianco, M.: ReaderBench: An Integrated Cohesion-Centered Framework. In: 10th European Conf. on Technology Enhanced Learning, Vol. LNCS 9307, pp. 505–508. Springer, Toledo, Spain (2015)
20. Dascalu, M., Dessus, P., Bianco, M., Trausan-Matu, S., Nardy, A.: Mining texts, learner productions and strategies with ReaderBench. In: Peña-Ayala, A. (ed.) Educational Data Mining: Applications and Trends, pp. 345–377. Springer, Cham, Switzerland (2014)
21. Dascalu, M.: Analyzing discourse and text complexity for learning and collaborating, Studies in Computational Intelligence, Vol. 534. Springer, Cham, Switzerland (2014)
22. Dumais, S.T.: Latent semantic analysis. Annual Review of Information Science and Technology, 38(1), 188–230 (2004)
23. Blei, D.M., Ng, A.Y., Jordan, M.I.: Latent Dirichlet Allocation. Journal of Machine Learning Research, 3(4-5), 993–1022 (2003)
24. Swoboda, T., Hemmje, M., Dascalu, M., Trausan-Matu, S.: Combining Taxonomies using Word2vec. In: DocEng 2016, pp. 131–134. ACM, Vienna, Austria (2016)
25. Koch, G.G.: Intraclass correlation coefficient. In: Kotz, S., Johnson, N.L. (eds.) Encyclopedia of Statistical Sciences, Vol. John Wiley & Sons, pp. 213–217. John Wiley & Sons, New York, NY (1982)

The effects of student interaction with blog-based course content on learning performance

Benazir Quadir[1,*], Jie Chi Yang[2], Jun Zhang[1], and Houli Gao[1]

[1] Information Management Department, Shandong University of Technology
benazir.quadir@gmail.com, zhangjun@sdut.edu.cn, sdutghl@163.com
[2] Graduate Institute of Network Learning Technology, National Central University, Taiwan
yang@cl.ncu.edu.tw

Abstract— Due to the huge growth in online learning, educators are demanding to use advanced software or social sites as online learning settings. However, they must consider how interaction with online course content impacts learning outcomes while using the unique features of software and social cites. Yet, understanding the effects of learner-content interaction on learning outcomes in blog-based learning environments is very few. Therefore, this study aims to investigate the effects of learner's interaction with blog based learning content on learning outcome. Two research questions were tested, and data were analyzed using regression analysis. The results show that learner-content interaction is essential for learning output, and a significant relationship was found. A subsequent analysis showed that there is a significant relationship in learning performance between students' subjective and objective learning outcomes.

Keywords: Learner-content interaction; learning performance; blog-based learning

1 Introduction

Real learning environments can be achieved by adopting quality interactive approaches in online courses. Quality interactivity must be designed to support learning objectives and the interface and infrastructure that support the content [1], which are the primary drivers of the development of online courses [2]. Many online courses which provide learner-content facilitate the use of interactive tools such as electronic bulletin boards, discussion boards, email, and synchronous chat areas. The success of online courses mainly depends upon understanding how the learners engage in and interact with the course content. Educational applications require higher degrees of multimedia-based learner-content interaction in order to enhance learning performance [3], interest and motivation [4]. Thus, learner-content interaction is needed for effective instructional practice and individual discovery [5]. Therefore, researchers are mainly focused on the term "interaction" when implementing online courses.

Educators use the term interactivity to describe the degree of learners' intellectual, emotional, and physical engagement with the learning content [6]. Despite abundant evidence for the necessity of learner-content interaction, it is arguably one of the neglected components in online learning systems which use blogs. For a blog system to be cognitively effective, active comments on the content must be fostered. On the other hand, reflective experiences on learning content on blogs by the learners should also be stimulated to help them internalize the knowledge they have acquired so as to promote deep learning. However, the effects of learner-content interaction in blog-based learning environments on learning outcomes are still unclear. Therefore, this study examines student patterns of access to course content on learning performance to provide insights into the way in which course materials are used in a blog-based course as well as influence on learning outcomes. Moreover, the current study presents the research literature and validates the relative importance of learning outcomes attained from the blog-based learning experience. Thus, the present study specifically designed a weblog system named "Learner's Digest Blog" (LDB) as the chief source of learner-content interaction for a graduate level university course in which the students can initiate discussion on specific topics relevant to the subject of inquiry, read content thoroughly, share ideas, construct knowledge, and respond and react to others' content-based posts, all of which can support a productive learning environment. Therefore, the importance of this study lies in examining the students' experiences as blog-based learners on learning outcomes, thereby helping understand student perceptions of blog content interaction so that better educational environments and learning outcomes can be provided for online learners using blogs.

Through one semester observation of the interactivity between the learners and content during the course (i.e., the Weblog system incorporated into the course), and analyzing the data collected in the form of weblog posts, chat logs and exam scores, we attempt to answer the following two research questions:

1. How does the learner-content interaction affect learning performance in the blog-based course?
2. Are there any differences between learners' subjective and objective learning outcomes in the blog-based learning environment?

2 Literature review

2.1 Learner-content interaction in blog-based learning environments

Interaction is considered a central part of virtually any educational experience. Wagner [7] defined interaction in distance education contexts as "reciprocal events that require at least two objects and two actions. Inter-actions occur when these objects and events mutually influence one another" (p. 8). While this definition captures the reciprocity of interaction which invariably involves the interplay between at least two actors (either objects or actions), it does not differentiate the modality of various forms of interaction occurring in online learning contexts. Emphasizing dialogue and structure in the transactional distance of distance education, Moore [8] classified interaction into three types, learner-content interaction, learner-teacher interaction, and learner-learner interaction. These types of interaction are present in all learning systems, whether delivered over a distance or on campus. In this study, we chiefly examine the effect of interaction between learner and content arising from participation in a blog-based course by considering one of the three forms of interaction identified by Moore [8].

Learner-content interaction is defined as a process of "intellectually interacting with content to bring about changes in the learner's understanding, perspective or cognitive structures" (p. 2) [8]. It occurs when learners utilize interactive tools such as audio, video, text, and graphic representations during course study [9]. Numerous studies have identified the positive relationship between online learning and student interactivity with course contents [10; 11], but most content developers and educators seem not to entirely apply the unique features of blog-based online learning. However, content-based learning in various forms of presentation and instructional design strategies need to be carefully planned in the blog-based learning environment.

Current weblog systems are regularly updated web pages which include journal-like text entries, pictures and other multimedia content [12] as well as an information retrieval option to retrieve the necessary resources relevant to the topic [13]. Moreover, reading blogs allow learners to interact with the content [5] and connect with the learning environment. For example, a student/teacher may publish an article/course-content or even a few lines of random thoughts on the subject of inquiry, then other students may respond to the article by giving comments and following the discussion thread. Commenting on articles/course-content is a way of conversing with other learners and the whole learning community for reflective dialog and learning support.

2.2 Learner-content interaction on learning performance

Numerous studies have found that learner-content interaction has an influence on learning [14; 15; 16]. As Reisetter, LaPointe, and Korcuska [17] found, online learners ranked learner-content variables as having the highest importance in online settings, and content is the general locus where new knowledge, skills, and abilities are presented [15]. Interactive content representations could help students comprehend text, and could motivate them to learn [16]. However, lacking motivation to read the course content causes students to drop out [18]. Therefore, content presentation is not only important but is in fact one of the critical variables affecting learning effectiveness [11]. In the LDB blog, content presentation is articulated with text and graphics, interactive text and graphics, and interactive multimedia, as Belanger and Jordon [19] suggested that these three approaches are needed for learning when taking online courses. When more learner-content interaction arises in multimedia-based e-learning environments, then learning performance and learner satisfaction can be enriched [14].

3 Technical forum of Interactivity – A LDB blog function

In order to achieve interactivity goals between learner-content, interactive technical functions need to be designed in blog-based learning systems. For example, to facilitate learner–content interaction by providing more content choices, designers can set presentation links to related learning contents on the Web [20]. This study used interactive functions, interactive analysis and instructional necessity level associated with learner-content, adopted respectively from Chou [20], slightly modified to adjust to the present researcher's experience with blog-based learning system design as shown in Table 1.

Table 1. Dimensions, interactive functions and instructional necessity level of learner-content interaction

Dimensions of interactivity	Interactive functions in learning blog systems	Instructional necessity level
Choice	Links to related educational sites/social sites	Recomended
Non-sequential access of choice	Links to related learning materials	Recomended
Adaptability	Individual learning portfolio on blog Read blog-content thoroughly	Compulsory Compulsory
Responsiveness to users	Power-point slide submission on blog	Compulsory
Ease of adding information	Learner contributing to learning material Post sharing Follow by e-mail	Compulsory Compulsory Optional
Encourage learner to post best writing	Most popular post provided by learners are announced with a reward/gift	Encouraged

Each student was required to post at least two posts related to the lecture topic, and update information after the lectures.

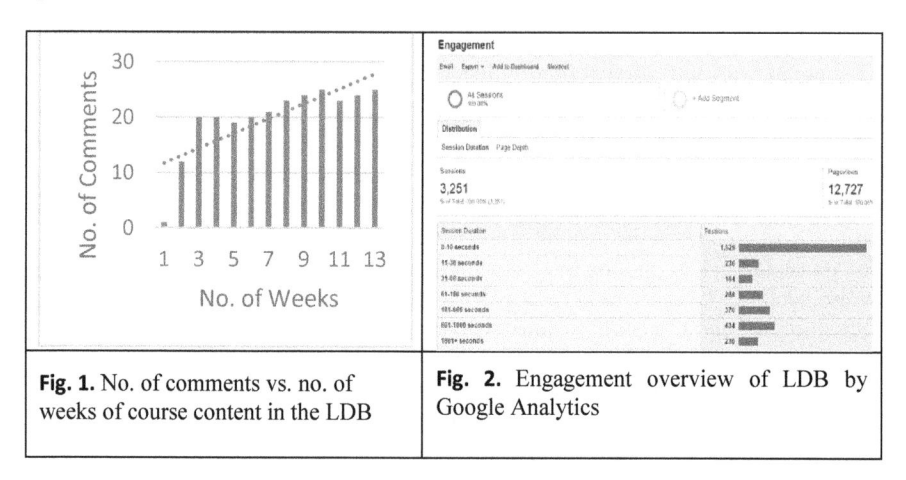

Fig. 1. No. of comments vs. no. of weeks of course content in the LDB

Fig. 2. Engagement overview of LDB by Google Analytics

Once they got the weekly course content of the blog they were required to read, comment on the content, and share their thoughts and idea. The number of comments for each week of course content in the LDB is shown in Fig. 1. By commenting in this way, the learners not only maintained good communication with their classmates, but also enhanced their knowledge by interacting with the content. The engagement overview by session wise with page views is shown in Fig. 2. The "Learner's Digest" blog uses search engine optimization (SEO) to improve the visibility of the blog site. The content performance of the blog is tracked by Google Analytics (Fig. 3). The screen shot includes three interactions (pages). Each page is grouped into columns based on what stage of the process a learner is at, with the learner's point of entry on the left and progression moving toward to the right. In all, 53.1% of traffic abandons the site (bounces) after viewing the landing page. Popular landing pages are course content. In this figure the drop-offs become fewer and fewer as the learners progress through the 1st, 2nd, and 3rd interactions. Most learners who went all the way through the 3rd interaction viewed the course content which was uploaded weekly.

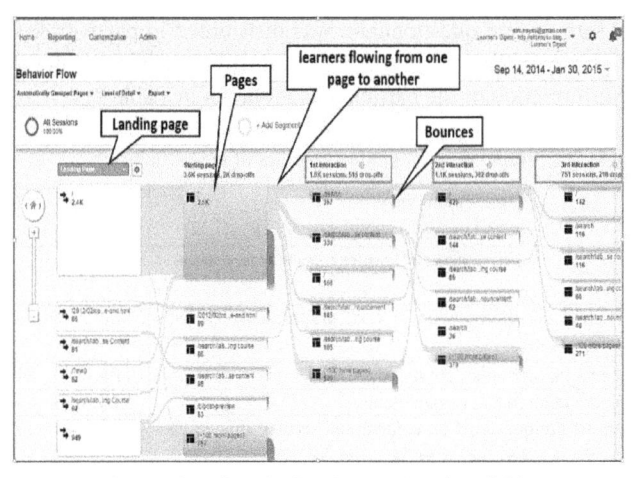

Fig. 3. Learner-content interaction flow in the "Learner's Digest" blog

4 Methods

4.1 Instruments

A questionnaire was developed to survey performance, learner-content interaction and learning outcomes (i.e., subjective and objective). The questionnaire is divided into five sections to specifically address the two research questions formulated in the study. Section one contains three questions capturing the respondents' demographic information such as age, gender and education. Section two contains three questions capturing their adopting time of computers, the Internet and experience of blog usage. Section three was developed for identifying learner content interaction with a six-question format. Section four contains six items that were used for identifying subjective learning outcome. Each item was rated on a five-point Likert scale, ranging from 1 (strongly disagree) to 5 (strongly agree). Finally, objective learning outcome was assessed by the examination including blog-based activities such as posting content, commenting on others' posts and assessing other posts constituted 20% of the final score, while midterm and final reports constituted 15% and 35%, respectively.

4.2 Participants and data collection

To obtain the sample, the questionnaire was distributed in paper-based format in a renowned university of Taiwan. A total of 26 students participated in this study. The demographic information of the participants is shown in Table 2.

Table 2. Demographic profiles and descriptive statistics of the participants

Name of the items	Mean	Stdv	FL
Items of learner content interactions			
LC1: I can access the presentation of text, graphics, animation, audio, video, etc.	4.46	.508	.788
LC2: I can access tailored instructional materials for my needs.	4.08	.845	N/A
LC3: I can access tailored test or quiz items.	4.00	.849	N/A
LC4: I can report my questions on content and receive immediate on-line help.	4.19	.567	.755
LC5: I can provide related links which contain useful information for the course.	4.15	.881	.696
LC6: I can participate in the events held, attracted and encouraged by special incentives, for example, a prize for the student who provides more interesting posts.	4.15	.543	.774
Items of learning outcomes			
LO1: Using the "Learner's Digest" blog improved my knowledge of digital learning courses including different digital learning topics.	4.42	.578	.848
LO2: I acquired some useful knowledge through interacting with other users on the "Learner's Digest" blog.	4.19	.694	.836
LO3: Engaging in the activities within the "Learner's Digest" blog context enhanced my skills of using Web 2.0 applications.	3.96	.774	.778
LO4: I was very satisfied with the "Learner's Digest" blog.	4.12	.766	.817
LO5: While participating in the "Learner's Digest" blog, I experienced a sense of pleasure.	4.12	.864	N/A
LO6: It is worth participating in the "Learner's Digest" blog.	4.23	.765	.807

4.3 Assessing reliability and validity

In this study, there were 4 items for learner content interaction, and the reliability of these items is .715. For the subjective learning outcome construct there were 5 items, the reliability of which is .811. The internal consistency for all constructs was decided according to Cronbach's alpha. With the range of alpha scores from .715 to .811 obtained in this study, we can conclude that the questionnaire is reliable and that the data are suitable for analysis.

To achieve construct validity, the data were examined using principal component analysis as the extraction technique and varimax as the method of rotation. With a cut-off loading of 0.50 and an eigenvalue greater than 1.0, three of the items were dropped. The results of the exploratory factor analysis revealed that the factor loading of items varied from 0.696 to 0.848 as shown in Table 3.

Table 3. The descriptive statistics and the factor loadings of the items

Characteristics	Categories	Frequency	Percentage (%)
Gender	Male	15	57.7%
	Female	11	42.3%
	Total	26	100
Age	Less than 25	21	80%
	25-35	4	16%
	More than 35	1	4%
	Total	26	100
Education	Graduate	20	76.9%
	PhD	6	23.1%
	Total	26	100
Internet user	≤ 2000	8	30.76%
	2001 to 2005	11	42.30%
	≥2006	7	26.92%
Computer user	≤2000	11	42.30%
	2001 to 2005	11	42.30%
	≥2006	4	15.38%
Blog usage experience	≤ 2000	4	15.38%
	2001 to 2005	8	30.76%
	≥2006	14	53.84%

5 Results

5.1 The effect of learner-content interaction on subjective learning outcome

A regression analysis was performed, with the measure of interaction between learner-content as the independent variable and that of subjective learning output as the dependent variable. The result of the regressions is presented in Table 4. Learner-content is a significant predictor of learning outcome (F[1, 24] = 16.140 p < .05). The squared multiple correlation coefficient, R^2, was 40%, which means the learner-content interaction could account for 40% of the subjective learning outcome of the blog-based online course. It was found that the learner-content interaction significantly predicted the subjective learning outcome (β=.634, p < .01).

Table 4. The regression results

Model	SS	Df	MS	F	Sig
Regression	3.150	1	3.150	16.14	.001
Residual	4.684	24	.195		
Total	7.834	25			

IV = Learner-content interaction, DV = Subjective learning outcome

5.2 The effect of learner-content interaction on objective learning outcomes

A regression analysis was used, with the measure of interaction between learner-content as the independent variables and that of objective learning output as the dependent variable. The result of the regressions is presented in Table 5. Learner-content is a significant predictor of learning outcome (F[1, 24] = 4.57 p < .05). The squared multiple correlation coefficient, R^2, was 16%, which means the learner-content interaction could account for 16% of the objective learning outcome. It was found that the learner-content interaction significantly predicted the subjective learning outcome (β=-.400, p < .05).

Table 5. The regression results

Model	SS	Df	MS	F	Sig
Regression	68.51	1	68.515	4.57	.043
Residual	359.43	24	14.97		
Total	427.94	25			

IV = Learner-content interaction, DV = Objective learning outcome

5.3 The relationship between subjective and objective learning outcomes in the blog-based online course

Table 6 shows that there was a correlation between objective learning outcome (M=81.02 SD =4.63) and subjective learning outcome (M =4.18, SD =.560), r =.41, p = < .05.

Table 6. The results of Pearson correlation between learning performance of subjective and objective outcomes in the blog-based online course

	Subjective learning outcome	Objective learning outcome
Subjective learning outcome Pearson Correlation	1	.418*
Sig.(2-tailed)		.033
N	26	26

6 Discussion and conclusion

This study investigated how learners' interaction with blog-based learning content associated with unique features of learning materials on learning output, and reported the results of the analysis of these research questions. It has been shown that learner-content interaction plays a role in predicting learning output. The result of this study is similar to the result of [10;11]. In terms of learning output, learner content interaction show significant influence on both subjective and objective learning output. This study also identifies that there is a significant positive relationship in learning performance between students' subjective and objective learning outcomes. It is possible because of effective interaction with sound pedagogical principles underlying the blog-based content design. For example, this study offers blog-content on the cognitive processes of learning with various types of learner-content interactivity in terms of multiple representations such as online content in text format with colors and subheadings, various types of hyperlinks, and interactive activities with feedback and interactive multimedia components such as video clips, PowerPoint slides etc. Such factors are very important for effective learning with a deep understanding of the learning materials. Moreover, Wang, & Newlin [18] found that the drop-off rate is higher if course contents fail to motivate good learning motivation. However, the learners who spend more time on blog have lower drop-off rate. In this study, Google Analytics shows that those learners who went all the way through the 3rd interaction viewed the course content which was uploaded weekly with a low drop-off rate. The findings of this study may help educational blog designers to create more effective learning content. For learners perspective this study may suggest to more learning–content interaction by providing comments, share idea, critics others post to enhance knowledge and reduce course drop rate. Institutions also may benefit to implement a blog-based learning along with traditional learning system. One of the limitation of this study is general finding were supported by 26 university level students who enrolled for same course work, so the results may not be generalized. Future study may consider different demographic with wide range of learner group.

References

[1] French, D. (1999). Internet based learning: An introduction and framework for higher education and business. Stylus Publishing, LLC.
[2] Brooks, M. (2009). The Excellent Inevitability of Online Courses. Chronicle of Higher Education, 55(38).
[3] Zhang, D. (2005). Interactive multimedia-based e-learning: A study of effectiveness. The American Journal of Distance Education, 19(3), 149-162.
[5] Deng, L., & Yuen, A. H. (2009). Blogs in higher education: Implementation and issues. TechTrends, 53(3), 95.
[4] Choi, H. J., & Johnson, S. D. (2005). The effect of context-based video instruction on learning and motivation in online courses. The American Journal of Distance Education, 19(4), 215-227.
[5]. Sim R (1997) Interactivity: a forgotten art? Computers in Human Behavior 13, 2, 157–180.
[6] Yacci, M. (2000). Interactivity demystified: A structural definition. Educational Technology, 40(4), 5-16.
[7] Wagner, E. D. (1994). In support of a functional definition of interaction. American Journal of Distance Education, 8(2), 6–26
[8] Moore, M.G. Three types of interaction. American Journal of Distance Education, 3 (2), 1-6, 1989.
[9] Hirumi, A. (2006). Analysing and designing e-learning interactions. In C. Juwah (Ed.), Interactions in online education: Implications for theory and practice (pp. 46-71). New York: Routledge.
[10] Ellis, R. A., Ginns, P., & Piggott, L. (2009). E-learning in higher education: Some key aspects and their relationship to approached to study. Higher Education Research & Development, 28(3), 303-318.
[11] Allen, M. W. (2003). e-Learning: Building interactive, fun, and effective learning programs for any company. Hoboken, NJ: Wiley.
[12] Quadir, B, & Chen, N, S. (2015). The effects of reading and writing habits on blog adoption. Behaviour &Information Technology, 34(9).
[13] Te Wang, K., Huang, Y. M., Jeng, Y. L., & Wang, T. I. (2008). A blog-based dynamic learning map. Computers & Education, 51(1), 262-278.
[14] Zhang, D. (2005). Interactive multimedia-based e-learning: A study of effectiveness. The American Journal of Distance Education, 19(3), 149-162.
[15] Northrup, P. T. (2002). Online learners' preferences for interaction. The Quarterly Review of Distance Education, 3(2), 219-226.
[16] Potelle, H., & Rouet, F. (2003). Effects of content representation and readers' prior knowledge on the comprehension of hypertext. International Journal of Human-Computer Studies, 58(3), 327-345.
[17] Reisetter, M., LaPointe, L., & Korcuska, J. (2007). The impact of altered realities: Implications of online delivery for learners' interactions, expectations, and learning skills. International Journal on E-Learning, 6(1), 55-80.
[18] Wang, A. Y., & Newlin, M. H. (2002). Predictors of web-student performance: The role of self-efficacy and reasons for taking an online class. Computers in Education, 18(2), 151-163.
[19] Belanger, F., & Jordan, D. H. (2000). Evaluation and implementation of distance learning: Technologies, tools and techniques. Hersey, PA: Idea Group.
[20] Chou, C. (2003). Interactivity and interactive functions in web - based learning systems: a technical framework for designers. British Journal of Educational Technology, 34(3), 265-279.

The *Objective Ear*: Assessing the Progress of a Music Task

Joel Burrows[1] and Vivekanandan Kumar[2]
Athabasca University
joelburrows@outlook.com, vive@athabascau.ca

Abstract. Music educators assess the progress made by their students between lessons. This assessment process is error prone, relying on skills and memory. An *objective ear* is a tool that takes as input a pair of performances of a piece of music and returns an accurate and reliable assessment of the progress between the performances. The tool evaluates performances using domain knowledge to generate a vector of metrics. The vectors for a pair of performances are subtracted from each other and the differences are used as input to a machine-learning classifier which maps the differences to an assessment. The implementation demonstrates that an *objective ear* tool is a feasible and practical solution to the problem of assessment.

Keywords: Music education, assessment, learning analytics, machine learning.

1 Introduction

We define an *objective ear* as an agent that takes as input a pair of performances of a piece of music and returns an accurate and reliable classification of the progress made between the two performances. For example, a student at a music lesson may perform a piece that he or she is working on and the agent will compare that performance to the performance from the previous lesson and determine that the student has made no progress between lessons. Teachers and students can use such a tool as feedback during a music lesson, but the tool could also be used as part of a learning environment to provide valuable information to educators on the conditions under which a student makes progress. This paper describes the successful implementation of an *objective ear*.

2 Background

A music teacher's ability to assess students has been well researched. The type of training a music teacher receives affects the kinds of errors a teacher detects. For example, band teachers are more attuned to rhythm errors whereas choir teachers are more attuned to pitch errors [13]. Several factors affect a teacher's ability to detect a pitch error, such as the size of the interval between a pitch and the previous pitch [6]. Discrepancies in assessment arise when assessing the performance of an entire piece of music compared to splitting it into pieces and evaluating each section individually [2]. Thus, an *objective ear* fulfills a need to aid teachers in performing accurate assessments.

An *objective ear* must be matched to a genre of music. A universal objective ear is impossible because the fundamental rules of music have changed over time, and vary across the music traditions of various cultures. For this implementation of an objective ear, we limited the scope to Western music from the Classical era. This era covers the rise of Haydn and continues through to the death of Beethoven, roughly a period between the late 1700s and the early 1800s [7].

3 Method

The *objective ear* has two main components: an evaluator and a classifier. Two performances of a piece of music in the MIDI data format [8] are input to the evaluator component. The evaluator performs several analyses of these performances. Each analysis results in a metric, and thus the evaluator produces a vector of metrics for each performance. These two vectors from the two performances are subtracted from each other, resulting in a difference vector. This difference vector is the input to a classifier that maps the difference vector to a classification from the set {*worse, same, better*}.

The evaluator applies a variety of techniques derived from the field of automated music analysis to create the metrics. From these analyses, we obtain the features used as input to the classifier. The evaluator does not rely on a score, but in the same way that a human familiar with a music tradition can detect errors in a piece that he or she has never heard before, the evaluator component identifies likely errors.

A tempo analysis determines the tempo of the piece of music. Often, as a student masters a task, the tempo of the student's performance increases, making the tempo a valuable metric for progress. To find the tempo, the inter-offset-interval (IOI) of every note is calculated. This is the duration between a note and its predecessor. Notes played simultaneously have an IOI time of zero. These zero IOIs are ignored, and the rest are clustered to find the largest cluster of IOIs using a hierarchical agglomerative clustering algorithm [3]. This method of finding the tempo does not reliably find the tempo as per the written score of a piece of music but rather a multiple of the written tempo; but the tempo remains accurate relative to other performances of the same piece of music, making it suitable as a metric.

A pitch analysis searches for likely pitch errors. The evaluator identifies pitch errors by applying a hidden Markov model using an n-Gram technique on a transformed data set to find unlikely pitch intervals. It transforms the data into an appropriate alphabet by first categorizing notes as being long, medium, short or simultaneous, based on the tempo of the piece. Rather than processing raw pitches, it extracts the interval between two pitches and scales it to an octave. For example, if a note with a long inter-offset-interval moves from C to E, in this alphabet it is represented as a long major third. Thus, the alphabet consists of pairs of durations and intervals.

The n-Gram approach to finding pitch errors requires a dataset for training. The training data comes from Classical piano music transformed into the pitch analyzer's alphabet. The pitch analyzer uses this data to calculate the probabilities of 3-grams. After converting a performance to our alphabet, the evaluator determines the likelihood of a note given its predecessors. The evaluator flags improbable notes – sequences of three notes for which their 3-gram probability is below a configurable threshold – as being unlikely. By dividing the number of likely errors by the number of notes, the evaluator calculates a normalized error rate for pitch errors.

The rhythm analysis applies the tempo analysis to find likely rhythm errors. Rhythm in the Classical period is usually related to the tempo by a factor of two or three. The evaluator first derives all expected inter-onset-intervals for notes by multiplying and dividing the tempo by integers whose factors contain only two or three. It then compares the actual inter-onset-interval for each note to the closest value in the set of expected IOIs and determines which notes deviate too much from any of the expected values, the amount of deviation being a configurable parameter. As with the pitch errors, the evaluator divides the number of rhythm deviations by the total number of notes to give a normalized error rate for rhythm errors.

This approach is unnecessarily broad because a performer can slightly change the tempo of a piece of music during a performance. A piece of music can, structurally, be broken recursively into smaller sections. At the end of more significant sections, it is acceptable in much of Western music for the performer to slow the tempo. The evaluator analyzes the piece to find the various sections [9] and based on how close a note is to the end of a major section, it allows the note to deviate more from the expected note value. Like the rhythm analysis, this gives us rhythm errors which we turn into a normalized error rate.

Performers of music from the classical period frequently decorate the music with ornaments. Ornaments are musical figures that a performer typically plays very quickly, but identifying ornaments is difficult because they inherently ambiguous depending on how the composer notates the music. The evaluator considers all short passages of quick notes that do not deviate too much from a central pitch as an ornament, an approach similar to how we might identify ornaments when listening to a performance. This definition is sufficient to capture most ornaments. Using this rule-based approach, ornaments can be identified [5]. Once identified, we can categorize the number of ornaments and their complexity by counting the number of notes in an ornament. Using the complexity as a weight we can give a weighted count of ornaments in a piece and then normalize it to a rate. Unlike error rates, a higher value in the metric demonstrates greater mastery.

A final metric is created by grouping errors together. This approach is based on an intuitive examination of error detection. If a performer plays a note that is both the wrong pitch and rhythm, the listener may hear these as a single error. The evaluator groups errors in time. That is, all errors within a time threshold are combined as a single error. Using this approach, the evaluator counts the number of error groups, and normalizes this to an error rate per note.

For each performance, the evaluator component creates a vector of metrics. It subtracts the vectors for a pair of performances creating a difference vector. The classifier maps the difference vector to an indication of progress. A machine learning classifier requires a dataset for training, and the creation of such a dataset is part of this research activity. The dataset was prepared by recording pairs of performances of music from the Classical era. A set of eight human listeners listened to the pair of performances and classified the progress. By keeping the musical excerpts short, playing one excerpt immediately after the other, and using multiple listeners the dataset overcomes flaws in human assessment. In total, 227 pairs of performances were evaluated.

We chose a simple decision tree classifier that uses information gain to determine best split points because decision trees, as opposed to many other kinds of classifiers, can be analyzed to generate human-understandable rules. For teachers who are suspicious of an *objective ear*, being able to understand the rules used by the tool is important. The items in the dataset are randomly split between the training set and the test set with two-thirds of the items put in the training set and one third in the test set. This decision tree implementation did not perform any pruning.

4 Results

To test the classifier, and the overall system, we ran the items in the test set through the classifier, and compared the decision tree's classification to the expected classification from the human judgements. From this we created a confusion matrix for the classifier and in turn determined the classifier's accuracy. We also calculated the standard error of the classifier, and thus gave a confidence interval for the classifier's accuracy.

If we let T be the sum of the elements on the diagonal of the confusion matrix and n be the total number of data points, we calculate the accuracy as:

$$accuracy = \frac{T}{n}, \qquad (1)$$

the standard error as:

$$SE = \sqrt{\frac{accuracy(1-accuracy)}{n}}, \qquad (2)$$

and the 95% confidence interval as:

$$[accuracy - 1.96SE, accuracy + 1.96SE]. \qquad (3)$$

Other common machine learning measurements such as precision and recall are less important for the *objective ear* because false positives are just as problematic as false negatives.

Running the test set against the classifier produces:

Table 1. Confusion Matrix

	Worse	Same	Better
Worse	22	1	4
Same	1	28	6
Better	2	9	34

The accuracy is 0.785, the error rate is 0.215, and the standard error is 0.040. Applying the standard error, we get a 95% confidence interval with the range [0.707, 0.863].

An intermediate dataset was created by the evaluator processing the dataset's elements and pairing each resulting difference vector with its original element's judgement. Using the Weka toolset [4] a variety of classifiers were trained using this dataset, producing the following results:

Table 2. Weka Classifier Accuracy

Algorithm	Accuracy
J.48 Decision Tree	0.819
Random Forest	0.842
Multilayer Perceptron	0.853
Decision Table	0.864

5 Discussion

The results show that an *objective ear* is feasible. The implementation provides a tool sufficiently powerful to add value to a music learning system and aid students and teachers in music education. The experimentation with the Weka toolkit does show that the decision tree used in the tool is less accurate than other types of machine learning classifiers, indicating that tool could be improved by further tuning the decision tree or by choosing a different classification algorithm; but it also shows that the features extracted by the evaluator are sufficient to determine progress.

6 Conclusion

The *objective ear* is a powerful tool for music educators. This research demonstrates the feasibility of automating assessment. Possible next steps include extending the tool to support music from other periods of Western music, such as the Baroque and Romantic periods, or to support non-Western music traditions. As well, we could dramatically improve the tool's usability by applying automated music transcription to convert raw audio signals into MIDI data. The field of automated music transcription is still progressing, and may soon be able to accurately perform the necessary transcription. This would make it possible to implement the *objective ear* as a smartphone app, making it significantly easier to use and expanding the tool to instruments that do not provide MIDI interfaces.

The approach used by the *objective ear* could be applied to other performative skills such as dancing, figure skating, or boxing. In these cases, the evaluator's metrics would need to be implemented using domain specific analyses. For many of these skills, a tool that accurately assesses progress would provide value.

References

[1] Chordia, Parag, Avinash Sastry and Sertan Senturk. "Predictive Tabla Modelling Using Variable-length Markov and Hidden Markov Models." Journal of New Music Research, vol. 40, no. 2, pp. 105-118, 2011.

[2] Darrow, Alice-Ann. "Examining the validity of self-report: middle-level singers' ability to predict and assess their sight-singing skills." *International Journal of Music Education*, vol. 24, no. 1, pp. 21-29, 2006.

[3] Dixon, Simon. "Automatic Extraction of Tempo and Beat from Expressive Performances." Journal of New Music Research, vol. 30, no. 1, pp. 39-58, 2001.

[4] Eibe, Frank, Mark A. Hall, and Ian H. Witten. The WEKA Workbench. Online Appendix for "Data Mining: Practical Machine Learning Tools and Techniques", Morgan Kaufmann, Fourth Edition, 2016.

[5] Gingras, Bruno and Stephen McAdams. "Improved Score-performance Matching Using Both Structure and Temporal Information from MIDI Recordings." Journal of New Music Research, vol. 41, no. 1, pp. 43-57, 2011.

[6] Groulx, Timothy. "The Influence of Tonal and Atonal Contexts on Error Detection Accuracy." *Journal of Research in Music Education*, vol. 61, no. 2, pp. 233-243, 2013.

[7] Grout, Donald J. *A History of Western Music*. 6th ed. W. W. Norton & Company Inc., New York, NY. 2001.

[8] Guerin, Robert. *MIDI Power!*. 2nd ed. Cengage Learning. Boston, MA. 2008.

[9] Hamanaka, Masatoshi, Keiji Hirata, and Satoshi Tojo. "Implementing 'A Generative Theory of Tonal Music'." Journal of New Music Research, vol. 35, no. 4, pp. 249-277, 2006.

[10] Pearce, Marcus and Geraint Wiggins. "Improved Methods for Statistical Modelling of Monophonic Music." Journal of New Music Research, vol. 33, no. 4, pp. 367-385, 2004.

[11] Raphael, Christopher and Joshua Stoddard. "Functional Harmonic Analysis Using Probabilistic Models." Computer Music Journal, vol. 28, no. 3, pp. 45-52, 2004.

[12] Siemens, George. "Learning Analytics: The Emergence of a Discipline." American Behavioral Scientist, vol. 57, no. 10, pp. 1380-1400, 2013.

[13] Stambaugh, Laura. "Differences in Error Detection Skills by Band and Choral Preservice Teachers." *Journal of Music Teacher Education*, vol. 25, no. 2, pp. 25-36, 2016.

[14] Widmer, Gerhard. "Machine Discoveries: A Few Simple, Robust Local Expression Principles." Journal of New Music Research, vol. 31, no. 1, pp. 37-50, 2002.

Visualizing and Understanding Information literacy Research Based on the CiteSpaceV

Liqin Yu [1], Di Wu [2,*], Sha Zhu [1], and Huan Li [1]

[1] National Engineering Research Center for E-Learning, Central China Normal University, 430079, Wuhan, China
yu_liqin_hope@163.com

[2] Educational Informatization Strategy Research Base Ministry of Education, Central China Normal University, 430079, Wuhan, China
wudi@mail.ccnu.edu.cn
*Corresponding Author

Abstract. The aim of this study is to visualize the status quo of the research on information literacy via co-citation analysis. A total of 1326 papers with full bibliographic records were retrieved from Web of Science database as the sample. CiteSpaceV was used to conduct visualization analysis to build knowledge map by identifying the representative countries, research hotspots, evolution path and research frontiers in the field of information literacy.

Keywords: Information literacy. CiteSpaceV. Co-citation analysis.

1 Introduction

Since the 1990s, with the development and application of information technology, we gradually entered into the information society. Information literacy is as essential as basic reading and writing in the information society. The term "information literacy" was been firstly put forward by Zurkowski in 1974 .Then, information literacy has got more and more attention. In order to provide insights into research state about information literacy, this study aims to deeply analyze the core countries, research hotspots, research frontier and evolution path of information literacy by using the Cite Space V.

2 Research methodology

2.1 Research tool

Cite Space V[1] was choosed as the research tool in this study, which is a computer program developed in Java by Dr. Chen for visualizing and analyzing literature of a scientific domain. Cite Space V takes bibliographic information from the Web of Science and generates co-citation networks, nodes and links to summarize key information about the literature analyzed.

2.2 Data collection

The input data sources used in this paper come from the Web of Science database which is published by the Institute for Scientific Information (ISI). The data retrieval strategy is the following: Topic= Information literacy OR Computer literacy OR ICT literacy OR information competency; The scope of subject is limited in Computer Science, Education educational research, psychology, Telecommunication and other related education fields.

3 Research Results and Discussions

3.1 Analysis of core countries

We selected "country" as the "node type", set top N=50. Finally, the cooperation network of country was generated, as shown in Fig. 1.

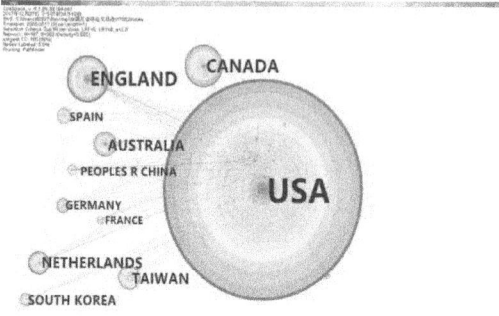

Fig. 1. Country distribution diagram of information literacy research

As can be seen from Table1 and Fig.1, in the field of information literacy research, USA occupied the top place with 554 pieces. England ranked the second place with the number of 118 pieces. The rest of rankings were Canada, Australia and so on. Since information literacy research started late relatively, China ranked 10th place with 32 pieces.

Table 1. Country distribution of information literacy research.

Rank	Literature Quantity	Country	Rank	Literature Quantity	Country
1	554	United States	6	61	New Zealand
2	118	England	7	48	Spain
3	105	Canada	8	41	Germany
4	67	Australia	9	33	Korea
5	63	Taiwan	10	32	China

3.2 Analysis of research hotspots

The high frequency keywords are often used to define a hot issue.[2] In this study, we select "keyword" and "term" as the node, use Pathfinder algorithm, and generate keywords co-occurrence graph and as it was shown in Fig 2.

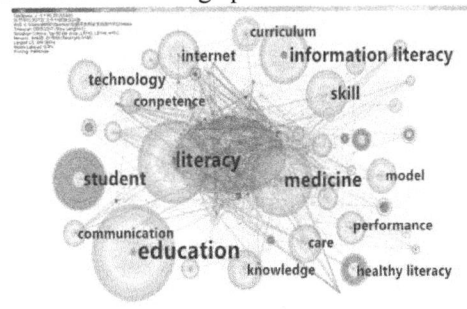

Fig. 2. Network map of research hot spots on information literacy

In Fig. 2, the ring represents keywords while the size of ring indicates their frequency, purple rings are key nodes, which mean mediation centricity greater than 0.1. It's not difficult to see that "education" was the highest frequency node.

Table 2. Hotspots on information literacy (frequency≥50).

Rank	Frequency	Keyword	Rank	Frequency	Keyword
1	179	education	8	83	technology
2	156	literacy	9	81	care
3	138	information	10	78	knowledge
4	118	student	11	71	model
5	115	Information literacy	12	70	curriculum
6	97	skill	13	70	performance
7	96	internet	14	65	health literacy

There are multiple hotspots from 2005 to 2017, such as education, literacy, skill , internet , technology , student , curriculum, knowledge , health literacy and so on. The top 14 high-frequency key words are listed in Table 2 whose frequency ≥ 50.

3.3 Analysis of research evolution path

The key node in network map is the node that owns the high degree of centrality or cited frequency [3]. The time Map of Information Literacy with 496 nodes and 962 lines as showed in Fig3.

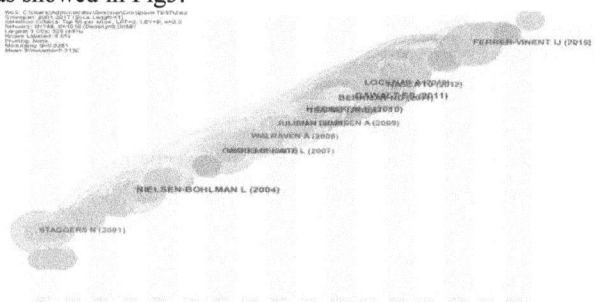

Fig. 3. High Cited Literature Time Map of Information Literacy

Based on the highly cited literatures, the authors classified the evolution path of "information literacy" into three stages:

— **First stage: The generation and connotation of "information literacy"**

Jan A.G.M. van Dijk (2003) published "The Deepening Divide: Inequality in the Information Society". he predicted that ultimately different uses of ICT will bring the most important digital and information inequalities in society.[4]David Bawden (2001) published "Information and digital literacies: a review of concepts". Related concepts, such as computer literacy, library literacy, network literacy, Internet literacy were described and reviewed by way of a literature survey and analysis.[5]

— **Second stage: Research and application of "information literacy" in the field of education**

Lina Markauskaite (2007) explored the structure of trainee teachers' ICT literacy including problem solving, communication and metacognition, basic ICT capabilities, analysis and production with ICT, information and Internet-related capabilities. [6]Amber Walraven (2008) proposed Children, teenagers and adults have trouble with specifying search terms and judging source and information, but schools and teachers has paid little attention to culture this skill embedded in curricula.[7]Heidi Julien examined the relationship between curricula in secondary-level science classrooms. The findings of this study demonstrated that many students lack of information search, analysis and evaluation of information skills.[8]

— **Third stage: The influential factors of "information literacy"**

AJAMV Deursen(2009) found that higher levels of education seem to perform best, age did not contribute to information skill related problems. [9]Meng-JungTsai(2009) investigated the gender differences in junior high school students' Internet self-efficacy and their behavior. The findings demonstrated girls had significant higher communicative Internet Self-Efficacy than had the boys, boys showed a significantly higher Internet use intensity than did the girls. [10]Eszter Hargittai (2010) proposed that higher levels of parental education, being a male, and being white or Asian American are associated with higher levels of Web-use skill. Additionally, socioeconomic status is an important predictor[11].

3.4 Analysis of research Frontier

In this study, the research frontiers are presented in Table 3 via the bursting detection algorithm.

Table 3. Bursts terms with regard to information literacy.

Rank	Bursts Terms	Bursts	Rank	Bursts Terms	Bursts
1	pedagogical issue	4.97	5	medical education	3.71
2	computer literacy	4.85	6	digital divide	3.69
3	medical	4.38	7	computer	3.68
4	learning	4.07	8	school	3.65
5	standard	3.75	10	worldwide web	3.65

From the table 3, we could see that "pedagogical issue", "learning"," medical education" "school" were the research frontiers of information literacy. In fact, with the rapid development of information technology, information literacy has got more and more attention in the field of education. many researchers conducted the research about integrating information technology into the curriculum with learning activities to cultivate students' information literacy[12, 13]. Additionally, "computer"," computer literacy", "standard" were the research frontiers of information literacy. In the early stage, information literacy was interpreted as the ability to use Computer. in November 2010, UNESCO put forward the standard of information literacy, including access/retrieve information; evaluate/understand information; use/create/exchange information[14].

4 Conclusions

This study takes information literacy as the subject and makes a visualized analysis based on the CiteSpaceV. This paper has presented core countries, research hotspots, research frontier and evolution path of information literacy. However, this study was limited to the database of WOS, the next study might carry out research of information literacy using different databases.

Acknowledgements. The work was supported by the Key Project of Philosophy and Social Science Research, "Internet +"Research on education system, Ministry of Education of China (16JZD043).

References

[1] Chen, C., Ibekwe-Sanjuan , F., Hou, J.: The structure and dynamics of cocitation clusters: A multiple‐perspective cocitation analysis. J. the Association for Information Science & Technology . 61, 1386–1409(2010)
[2] Chen, C.: CiteSpace II: Detecting and visualizing emerging trends and transient patterns in scientific literature. J. the Association for Information Science & Technology.57, 359-377(2006)
[3] Chen, C.: Searching for intellectual turning points: Progressive Knowledge Domain Visualization. the National Academy of Sciences, the United States of America (2004)
[4] Dijk, J.: The deepening divide :inequality in the information society. J. Mass Communication & Society. 11,221-234 (2003)
[5] Bawden, D.: Information and digital literacies: a review of concepts. J. Documentation. 57,218-259 (2001)
[6] Markauskaite, L.: Exploring the structure of trainee teachers' ICT literacy: the main components of, and relationships between, general cognitive and technical capabilities. J. Educational Technology Research & Development. 55,547-572 (2007)
[7] Walraven, A., Brand-Gruwel, S., Boshuizen, H.: Information-problem solving: A review of problems students encounter and instructional solutions. J. Elsevier Science.24,623-648 (2008)
[8] Julien,H. Barker, S.: How high-school students find and evaluate scientific information: A basis for information literacy skills development. J. Library & Information Science Research. 31, 12-17 (2009)
[9] Deursen, A., Dijk, J.: Using the Internet: Skill related problems in users' online behavior. J.Elsevier Science Inc.21,393-402(2009)
[10] Tsai, M. Tsai, C.: Junior high school students' Internet usage and self-efficacy: A re-examination of the gender gap. J. Computers & Education. 54, 1182-1192 (2010)
[11] Hargittai, E.: Digital Na(t)ives? Variation in Internet Skills and Uses among Members of the "Net Generation". J. Sociological Inquiry. 80, 92-113 (2010)
[12] Locknar, A., Mitchell, R., Rankin, J.: Survey Study of the Integration of Information Literacy Components into the First-Year Solid State Chemistry Course. J. the Optical Society of America. 56, 644-645 (2012)
[13] Gawalt, E.S., Adams, B.: A Chemical Information Literacy Program for First-Year Students. J. Chemical Education. 88, 402-407 (2011)
[14] UNESCO. Towards Media And Information Literacy Indicators , http://www.unesco.org/fileadmin/MULTIMEDIA/HQ/CI/CI/pdf/unesco_mil_indicators_background_document_2011_final_en.pdf

**Part II
Tutorial: Is Educational Research
a Matter of Digital Observations
and Data Balancing?**

Open Research and Observational Study for 21st Century Learning

Vivekanandan S. Kumar[*], Shawn Fraser, David Boulanger

Athabasca University, Alberta, Canada
{vivek, shawnf, dboulanger}@athabascau.ca

Abstract. Contemporary research practice unreasonably obscures formative research outcomes from public notice. Indeed, this exclusion -- often unintentional -- holds true even when the research is publicly funded. Accordingly, the Public must search scholarly channels, such as academic journals, for research information that is not composed for general comprehension. Essentially, a breach in information transmission separates researchers and society at large. In education, a similar communication gap exists between students and instructors, given that instructors rely on traditional assessment activities to measure student performance and rarely realize the corresponding study efforts. Consequently, certain important formative evidences go largely unnoticed. Today, researchers are exploring smart learning processes that exploit opportunities triggered by environmental affordance, personal need, and/or professional expectation, and mitigate various assessment difficulties.

This presentation introduces Open Research in the context of Smart Learning. First, it discusses the advantages of opening the research process to an authorized public, fellow students, educators and policymakers. For example, it argues that greater accessibility can promote research growth and integrity. Second, it uses observational study methods to illustrate the ways students and educators can conduct their own experiments using continuously arriving data. This second section introduces three matching techniques (i.e. Coarsened Exact Matching, Mahalanobis Distance Matching, and Propensity Score Matching) and three data imbalance metrics (i.e. L1 vector norm, Average Mahalanobis Imbalance, and Difference in Means) to assess the level of data imbalance within matched sample datasets. Ultimately, the presentation promotes Smart Learning Environments that incorporate automated tools for opportunistic capture, analysis and remediation of various formative study processes. Such environments can enable students to ethically share and receive study data that help them conduct personal observational studies on individual study related questions. Moreover, it explains key traits of observational studies that are relevant for smart learning environments, considering the comparable traits of blocked randomized experiments. Remarkably, this presentation proposes a novel idea to connect Open Research with Persistent Observational Study methods. It explores how open research can support adaptive and self-regulated learning. It advocates for innovative research practices that can produce better and smarter learning.

Keywords: matching in smart learning environments • propensity score matching • randomized experiment • interactive analysis • observational study • learning analytics • data imbalance • persistent observational study

1 Open Research

Typically, researchers do not publish their findings in formats that a Public can engage or understand; Worldwide, a critical communication gap divides research communities and the Public. Consequently, the Public remains largely uninformed about research outcomes, except for the little they can glean through popular media. Principally, researchers publish their outcomes in academic channels such as journals and conferences, which are meant for fellow researchers. Unfortunately, neither popular media nor scholarly publications capture the kinds of details about research processes that the Public can connect with. Given that society is usually on the receiving end of many research endeavors, it is concerning that it rarely participates in the research cycle – when researchers propose ideas, apply for funding, investigate ideas through various processes, reach outcomes, and drive new research directions. Accordingly, contemporary research practices appear to be unintentionally and unreasonably marginalizing public social awareness of research matters. This is an oversight that is especially striking for publicly funded research.

Certain data indicates that the Public wants to be involved in research. For instance, in a recent report on public attitudes towards research [15], 90 per cent of the sample population supported public involvement, while public trust in university researchers fluctuated between 60 and 90 per cent. This strongly suggests that an overwhelming majority of society wants to understand, question, utilize, influence, and engage in research processes -- especially when the research is publicly funded. Consequently, a compelling and justified opportunity emerges to cultivate a culture of open research that offers many benefits.

First, open research can empower the Public. Essentially, people can draw from direct involvement in evidence-based research for informed discussions on science, rather than relying on cultural beliefs, blind trust, basic intuition and media representations [16]. Second, greater public understanding can spark deeper research involvement, which is essential as many nations search to expand their researcher pool and regulate research spending [24, 25]. In addition, substantial public awareness of research processes will help the Public understand and value certain critical data, such as why the top 96 Canadian researchers [17] are among the top 1% researchers in the world. Thus, greater public participation could generate profound public interest to engage on a more fundamental and academic level. Third, Open Data [18, 19] allows for transparent sharing of information. For instance, Open Research welcomes investigative scrutiny by the Public, which ensures transparency in research processes. Accordingly, the Public can use open datasets to monitor ongoing research and perform various checks and balances, e.g. raise questions on research validity and applicability, lead audit studies on quality, and test outcomes for replicability. In this way, Open Science [20,21,23] can support the integrity and growth of science research. Fourth, open research can influence key marketplace and regulatory policies that promote positive public attitudes towards research, encourage richer participation and spark healthier competition in the private sector. In addition, greater believe in research integrity could further R&D investment by business enterprises. Moreover, improving public faith in research will help counter various concerning observations, such as those of a recent benchmark report [22] indicating a sharp reduction in business R&D expenditures as a share of GDP.

This presentation will deliberate the need for open research, including the need to encourage citizen engagement, to establish standards for open research, and to assess proposed policies to guide researchers in practicing open research. The next section discusses the merits of observational studies built on specific matching techniques.

2 Observational Study

Traditionally, the research community denotes randomized experiments as the gold standard [9-13] for science research. Nonetheless, completely randomized experiments have raised certain ethical concerns in educational settings. Accordingly, researchers are investigating observational studies [14] to supplement and possibly replace randomized experiments in educational research. Observational study refers to research that explores cause and effect whereby researchers limit their control of independent variables for ethical and logistical reasons. Nevertheless, many researchers believe that observational studies overestimate treatment effects, which can reduce their validity [10]. In addition, the results of observational studies may contain undetected confounding bias, thus leaving results open to debate. Essentially, several researchers maintain that the benefits of randomized experiments should not be oversimplified [11]. As a result, researchers are exploring the compatibility of both study types. Silverman [12] indicates that observational studies – using larger and more diverse population samples over longer follow-up periods -- can supplement the findings of randomized experiments.

This presentation proposes an observational study built on the matching techniques prescribed by King [8], in which increasingly available new sensors can better observe and/or record teaching and learning experiences in real-time. It will demonstrate how learning analytics processes can incorporate observational sensors and advance blocked randomized experiments that measure the impact of analytics. Ideally, such techniques could enable teachers to step into the roles of analytics researchers using Shiny's interactive analyses.

In addition, this presentation will explain matching techniques such as Propensity Score Matching [1], Coarsened Exact Matching [2], and Mahalanobis Distance Matching [3] along with their corresponding imbalance metrics, i.e. L1 vector norm, Average Mahalanobis Imbalance, and Difference in Means.

Propensity Score Matching is the most popular matching technique in observational studies [8]. This presentation will demonstrate its suboptimality by presenting an observational study with randomized and non-randomized data [4-6] using R libraries (MatchingFrontier [7], CEM, and MatchIt) and the web application framework for R called Shiny. It will measure the data imbalance accuracy of the proposed observational study design against an equivalent randomized experiment.

As mentioned above, this presentation aims to explore open research in the context of smart learning processes. This next section discusses some important features of Smart Learning and its relationship to open research.

3 Smart Learning

21st Century Smart Learning [26-29] exploits learning opportunities that are triggered by environmental affordance, personal need, and/or professional expectation. This presentation advocates for Smart Learning Environments to incorporate certain automated tools that enable the opportunistic capture, analysis and remediation of a learner's formative study processes [30]. Learning Analytics has tools to identify learning opportunities in the context of competence and pedagogy. This presentation will demonstrate a Learning Analytics system in the domain of 'computer programming' to measure the progress of students in various programming related competencies.

Success in learning depends on an awareness about adapting learning effectively, and self-regulated learning is key to that awareness. The presentation will demonstrate a computational model of self-regulation that tracks student ability to adapt their learning based on the outcomes of the model. In this way, learning analysis becomes more useful to students.

In addition, the presentation promotes learning environments that enable students to share and receive data arising from their study processes through a dynamic dashboard -- within an accepted ethical standard -- empowering them to conduct individual observational studies about their study related questions. Notably, research can benefit from wider scrutiny by being more open to an authorized public, fellow students, educators and policymakers. Moreover, students can share their Learning Analytics data with others. They can conduct their own observational studies and verify the utility of the self-regulation computational model using personal data and data from other students.

Smart Learning tools can assist students in conducting observational studies, especially in cases where the students may not be knowledgeable about the intricacies of observational studies. Specifically, many aspects of conducting an observational study can be automated within the learning environment itself, and students can utilize an automated toolkit for more vigorous study.

Typically, research studies -- longitudinal or otherwise -- have fixed timeframes, including a starting point and an ending point. This presentation will introduce participants to the possibility of conducting studies that are persistent in nature. Consequently, the study will continue to collect data and produce outcomes as and when various data become available. For example, self-regulation is an individual metacognitive trait of a student that has been shown to be instrumental to the academic performance of students. Studies of self-regulation have been conducted in specific domains (e.g., mathematics, study strategies, healthcare), on different participant profiles (e.g., K-5 students, higher education students), addressing many dependent variables (e.g., competency, memory, recall).

This presentation proposes Research Methods of Persistent Observational Study that can empower students to conduct observational studies and take on researcher roles in an open research system. In a persistent observational study on self-regulation the following variables will drive the generation of data, among others -- a) the study habits of the participating student population, b) the willingness of the population to share data, and c) the pattern of participant consent to use or to withdraw data. Basically, this process will facilitate more accurate and continuous research outcomes, by keeping research questions well-defined but leaving the collection, verification, validation and analysis of data dependent on the arrival of data. Ultimately, this presentation aims to explore novel research methods that promote smarter learning and better learning environments.

References

[1] Olmos, A., & Govindasamy, P. (2015). Propensity Scores: A Practical Introduction Using R. Journal of MultiDisciplinary Evaluation, 11(25), 68–88.
[2] Iacus, S. M., King, G., Porro, G., & Katz, J. N. (2012). Causal inference without balance checking: Coarsened exact matching. Political Analysis, 1–24.
[3] King, G., Nielsen, R., Coberley, C., & Pope, J. E. (2011). Comparative Effectiveness of Matching Methods for Causal Inference. Unpublished Manuscript, 15, 1–26. http://doi.org/10.1.1.230.3451
[4] LaLonde, R. J. (1986). Evaluating the econometric evaluations of training programs with experimental data. The American Economic Review, 604–620.
[5] Dehejia, R. H., & Wahba, S. (1999). Causal effects in nonexperimental studies: Reevaluating the evaluation of training programs. Journal of the American Statistical Association, 94(448), 1053–1062.
[6] Dehejia, R. H., & Wahba, S. (2002). Propensity score-matching methods for nonexperimental causal studies. Review of Economics and Statistics, 84(1), 151–161.
[7] King, G., Lucas, C., & Nielsen, R. (2014). The Balance-Sample Size Frontier in Matching Methods for Causal Inference. American Journal of Political Science.

[8] King, G., & Nielsen, R. (2016). Why propensity score should not be used for matching, (617).
[9] Hannan, E. L. (2008). Randomized Clinical Trials and Observational Studies: Guidelines for Assessing Respective Strengths and Limitations. JACC: Cardiovascular Interventions, 1(3), 211–217. http://doi.org/http://dx.doi.org/10.1016/j.jcin.2008.01.008
[10] Concato, J., Shah, N., & Horwitz, R. I. (2000). Randomized, Controlled Trials, Observational Studies, and the Hierarchy of Research Designs. The New England Journal of Medicine, 342(25), 1887–1892.
[11] Medical Publishing Internet, Kent W. The advantages and disadvantages of observational and randomised controlled trials in evaluating new interventions in medicine. Educational article [Internet]. Version 1. Clinical Sciences. 2011 Jun 9. Available from: https://clinicalsciences.wordpress.com/article/the-advantages-and-disadvantages-of-1blm6ty1i8a7z-8/.
[12] Silverman, S. L. (2009). From Randomized Controlled Trials to Observational Studies. The American Journal of Medicine, 122(2), 114–120. http://doi.org/http://dx.doi.org/10.1016/j.amjmed.2008.09.030
[13] At Work, Issue 83, Winter 2016: Institute for Work & Health, Toronto.
[14] Sullivan, G. M. (2011). Getting Off the "Gold Standard": Randomized Controlled Trials and Education Research. Journal of Graduate Medical Education, 3(3), 285–289. http://doi.org/10.4300/JGME-D-11-00147.1
[15] Lindholm, M. (2015), Public Commitment to Research, VA Barometer 2015/16 – VA Report 2015:6, Vetenskap & Allmänhet, http://v-a.se/downloads/varapport2015_6_eng.pdf
[16] Pardo, R., Calvo, S. (2002), Attitudes toward science among the European public: a methodological analysis, Public Understand. Sci. 11, 155–195, https://www.upf.edu/pcstacademy/_docs/155.pdf
[17] http://www.stic-csti.ca/eic/site/stic-csti.nsf/eng/00088.html
[18] http://globalopendatainitiative.org/
[19] http://open.canada.ca/en/open-data
[20] https://english.eu2016.nl/latest/news/2016/04/05/eu-action-plan-for-open-science
[21] http://cos.io
[22] http://www.stic-csti.ca/eic/site/stic-csti.nsf/eng/00088.html
[23] http://open.gc.ca
[24] http://www.nstmis-dst.org/PDF/FINALRnDStatisticsataGlance2011121.pdf
[25] http://data.uis.unesco.org
[26] Giannakos, M., Sampson, D. G. and Kidzinski, L. (2016), Introduction to smart learning analytics: Foundations and developments in video-based learning, Smart Learning Environment, Vol. 3 No. 12, doi: 10.1186/s40561-016-0034-2
[27] Gros, B. (2016), The design of smart educational environments, Smart Learning Environment, Vol. 3 No. 15, doi: 10.1186/s40561-016-0039-x
[28] Kinshuk, Chen, N. S. and Cheng, I. L. (2016), Evolution is not enough: Revolutionizing current learning environments to smart learning environments, International Journal of Artificial Intelligence in Education, Vol. 26 No. 2, pp. 561–581.
[29] http://www.p21.org/our-work/p21-framework
[30] Kumar, V.S., Fraser, S.N., Boulanger, D. (2017). Discovering the predictive power of five baseline writing competences, Journal of Writing Analytics, 1 (1), pp. N/A, https://journals.colostate.edu/analytics/article/view/107.
[31] Bartling, S and Friesike, S. (2017), Opening Science, Springer Open, http://book.openingscience.org

Part III
2nd International Workshop on Technologies Assisting Teaching and Administration

An educational role-playing game for modeling the learner's personality

Mouna Denden[1], Ahmed Tlili[1], Fathi Essalmi[1], Mohamed Jemni[1]

[1]Research Laboratory of Technologies of Information and Communication and Electrical Engineering (LaTICE), Tunis national higher school of engineering (ENSIT), Tunisia

mouna.denden91@gmail.com
ahmed.tlili23@yahoo.com
fathi.essalmi@isg.rnu.tn
mohamed.jemni@fst.rnu.tn

Abstract. Recently, there has been an increasing interest in learner modeling in order to provide personalized computer based learning experiences. Generally, researchers and practitioners use questionnaires as a method to model learners, including their personalities, which can be time consuming and not motivating. Therefore, this paper presents a new approach for modeling the learner's personality, specifically introvert/extrovert, using an online educational game and Learning Analytics (LA) system.

Keywords: Learning Analytics. Educational Games. Learner's Personality. Learner Model.

1 Introduction

Learners have different individual characteristics and because of that, they behave differently in Computer Based Learning (CBL) [1]. "Personality" is one of the characteristics which is widely identified as an important indicator of individual differences [2]. To gather information about learners, including personality, researchers usually use an explicate method, namely questionnaires. Tlili, Essalmi, Jemni, Kinshuk, and Chen [1] found that the most used method to model the learners' personalities in CBL is questionnaires.

Questionnaires present statements that describe individuals and they can be typically too long and make learners stressed and not motivated [1]. In addition, Okda and Oltmanns [3] stated that questionnaires may not be the best method to use, since learners may try to look in an acceptable version when they feel that they are being assessed by others. To overcome this problem, it is possible to use an implicit method to model the learners' personalities based on their game behaviors using an LA system. Siemens [4] defined LA as "the use of intelligent data, learner-produced data, and analysis models to discover information and social connections, and to predict and advise on learning." Therefore, this paper presents an online educational game and LA system to implicitly model the learners' personalities, specifically the introvert/extrovert personality. Jung [5] considered introversion as people who move their energy towards their inner world of feelings and ideas, while, he considered extraversion as people who move their energy towards the external world of people and activities.

The rest of this paper is structured as follows: section 2 presents the game design, while section 3 focuses specifically on describing how this game is used as a learning and modeling tool of personality. Finally, section 4 concludes the paper and presents future directions based on this research.

2 Game Design

To model the learner's personality based on his/her game behaviors, a newly online Computer Architecture Game (CAG) was developed and deployed on an OVH web server. CAG is a role-playing game which aims to teach the computer architecture subject [6]. The main goal of the learner is to install the antivirus in the central computer of Kairouan city in order to bring it back to life. Learners can experience various learning activities while achieving the CAG goal. In particular, during the learning-playing process, the learners' game traces are stored in game variables then are automatically saved in MySQL database deployed on the OVH web server as well. This is done using typical client-server architecture with PHP scripts. The next section describes the CAG game and the way it is used as a learning tool as well as a modeling tool of the learners' personalities.

3 CAG Game

The learners start by choosing their game character to control within CAG. After that, in order to achieve the game goal and win, they have to finish five different learning quests, namely collecting coins, shooting, quiz, buying and battle [6]. For instance, Figure 1 shows a screenshot of the shooting learning activity interface. The learner will experience, during this activity, two types of magical power to shoot the correct answer of the question defined in the "Missions" box (using right and left mouse click) regarding the computer architecture subject. Every time a correct answer is shot, the learner gains bonus money.

An educational role-playing game for modeling the learner's personality 131

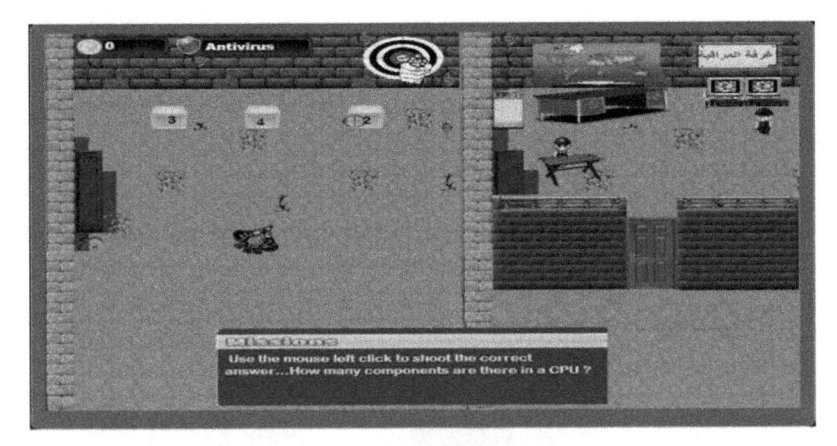

Fig. 1. Game interface of the "shooting" learning activity

Besides, the game also offers a simple and easy interface where teachers can update the delivered learning content to fit their next needs (e.g., the learning content can be updated to fit the next course chapter that the teacher wants to deliver to learners using CAG). This criterion allows the reusability of CAG with different learning contents. For example, Figure 2 shows a screenshot of the interface where he/she can modify the learning content of the "shooting" game activity. The teacher has to write in the first two text boxes (related to both magical powers using left and right mouse clicks) the questions that will appear to learners. In addition, he/she has to define the three answers, where learners should only shoot the correct answer among them. Finally, the teacher has to set the feedback message that will appear to learners in case the answer is correct or wrong.

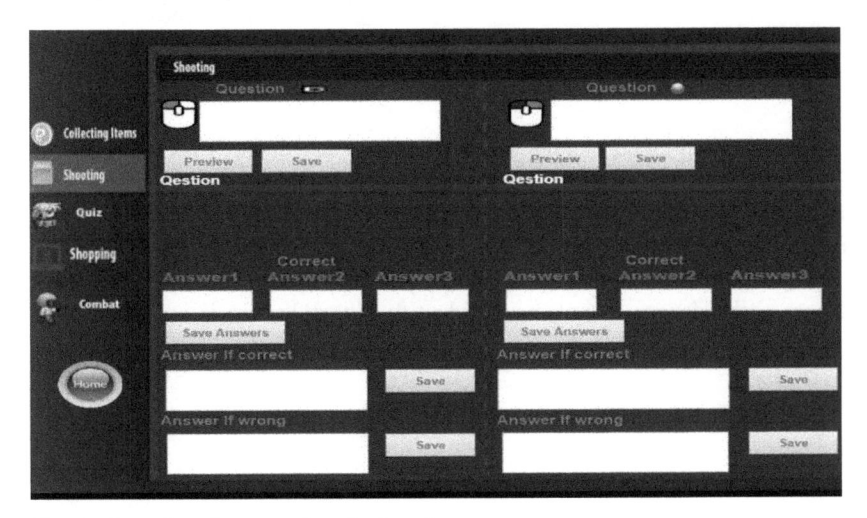

Fig. 2. Game interface to update the learning content

Furthermore, to model if learners have introvert or extrovert personalities, CAG implicitly collects the learners' traces using various game scenarios, during the learning-playing process. These traces were identified based on the extrovert/introvert features [7]. For instance, extroverts prefer hot colors while introverts prefer cool colors. Thus, the trace "Color" is used within CAG to see the type of color that the learner prefers [8]. Figure 3 presents the developed game scenario within CAG to implicitly collect this trace. In this context, the learners have to enter a clothes shop to pick up the clothes for their game characters which are available in two colors, namely red and sky blue. The choice of the learner can help to deduce if he/she is an extrovert or introvert. Of course, the game character's clothes will be changed to the selected color by the learner.

Fig. 3. CAG scenario to collect the "color" trace

Figure 4 also presents another game scenario to collect the "Risk" trace within CAG. In this context, extrovert people are known to be more risk takers than introvert people. Therefore, CAG presents two paths for learners, as shown in Figure 4. The one with the red arrow is written on it "dangerous", while the one with the green arrow is written on it "safe". The taken path can help to deduce if the leaner seeks danger or not, hence identify if that learner is an introvert or extrovert.

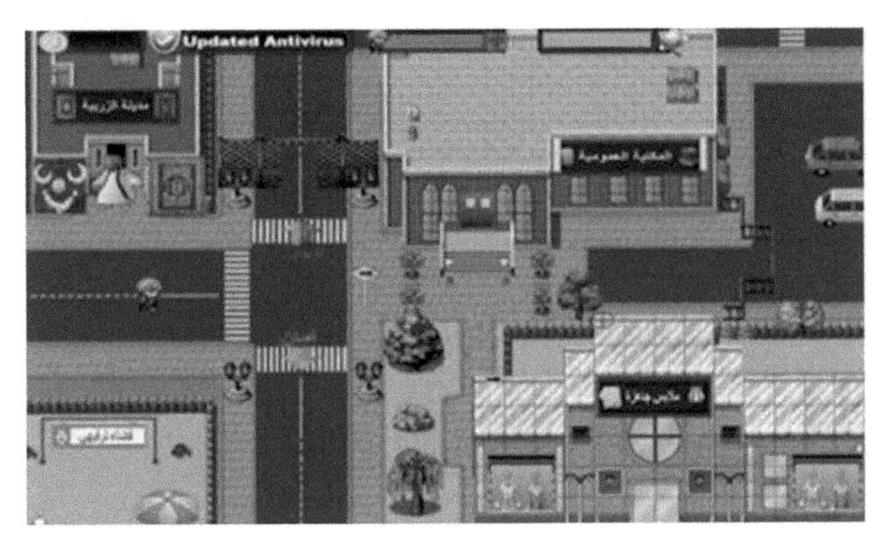

An educational role-playing game for modeling the learner's personality   133

Fig. 4. CAG scenario to collect the "risk" trace

Finally, the above presented traces (based on the game scenarios presented in Figure 3 and 4) were collected and fed to the developed LA system using C# language, based on the Naïve Bayes classifier, to identify each learner's personality, as shown in Figure 5. In this context, the obtained LA results can be used by teachers to provide personalized learning experiences to their learners according to their personalities.

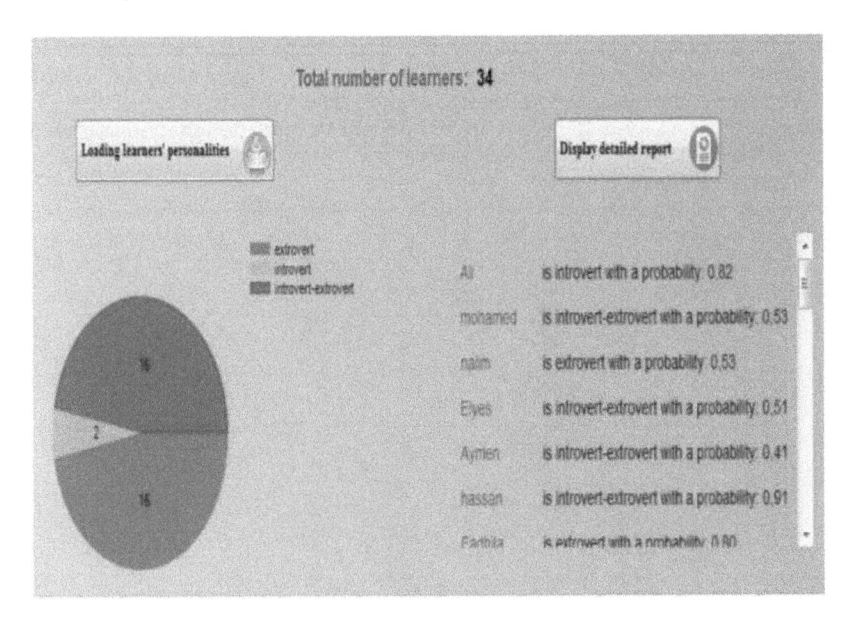

Fig. 5. Screenshot of the LA system results based on CAG

4   Conclusion

This paper presented two systems, namely an online educational game CAG and LA system, to implicitly model the learners' personalities, specifically the introvert/extrovert personality. In this context, the learners' traces were first collected from the CAG and then fed to the LA system. This system uses data mining techniques to model the learner's personality using Naïve Bayes classifier algorithm. Future directions could focus on: (1) Deploying both the LA system and CAG on the cloud to provide open learner model where it can be re-used by other learning systems; and, (2) Providing personalized learning-playing experiences within CAG based on each identified learner's personality.

References

[1] Tlili, A., Essalmi, F., Jemni, M., Kinshuk., Chen, N. S.: Role of personality in computer based learning. Computers in Human Behavior, vol. 64, pp. 805-813 (2016)
[2] Irani, T., Telg, R., Scherler, C., Harrington, M.: Personality type and its relationship to distance education students' course perceptions and performance. In Quarterly Review of Distance Education, 4(4), pp.445 (2003)
[3] Okada, M., Oltmanns, T. F.: Comparison of three self-report measures of personality pathology. Journal of Psychopathology and Behavioral Assessment, 31(4), 358-367, (2009)
[4] Siemens, G.: What are Learning Analytics?, Retrieved 7 December 2015 from http://www.elearnspace.org/blog/2010/08/25/what-arelearning-analytics/
[5] Jung, C. G., Baynes, H. G.: Psychological Types or the Psychology of Individuation. London: Kegan Paul Trench Trubner, (1921)
[6] Tlili, A., Essalmi, F., Jemni, M., Kinshuk.: An educational game for teaching computer architecture: Evaluation using learning analytics. In 5th IEEE International Conference on Information & Communication Technology and Accessibility (ICTA), pp. 1-6, (2015)
[7] Essalmi, F., Tlili, A., Ayed, L. J. B., Jemni, M.: Toward Modeling the learner's Personality using Educational Games. International Journal of Distance Education Technologies (IJDET), 15(4), 21-38 (2017)
[8] Serrano-Lagunaa, Á., Torrentea, J., Maneroa, B., del Blancoa, Á., Borro-Escribanoa, B., Martínez-Ortiza, I., Fernández-Manjóna, B.: Learning analytics and educational games: lessons learned from practical experience. In International Conference on Games and Learning Alliance, pp. 16-28 (2013)

Annotation Recommendation for Online Reading Activities

Miao-Han Chang[1], Maiga Chang[1*], Rita Kuo[2], Fathi Essalmi[3], Vivekanandan S. Kumar[1], Hsu-Yang Kung[4]

[1]Athabasca University, Canada
[2]New Mexico Institute of Mining and Technology, United States
[3]University of Kairouan, Tunisia
[4]National Pingtung University of Science and Technology
maiga.chang@gmail.com

Abstract. Both classroom and online learning ask students doing reading activities. The mature and widely used e-readers allow students reading and making annotation on the screen with their computer, tablet, or even smartphone. Annotations will be a very important resource aside from the notes for students while preparing for exams. However, sometimes students might think something is not important or relevant or just simply overlook while making annotations on the materials. Such annotations might lead to lose marks later when they are writing exams. The research team has developed an online annotation system that allows teachers to create online reading activities for their students and review students' annotations on the e-text. Moreover, with the help of a bio-inspired innovative clustering method GRACE (General Rapid Annotation Clustering Enhancement), students will be offered annotation recommendations based on the similarity their annotations have from other students on the same text. In such case, students may reconsider the content they chose to ignore or overlooked earlier and make their annotations more complete and better for exam preparation later..

Keywords: annotation, bio-inspired approach, clustering, e-text, recommendation

1 Introduction

Nowadays students are getting used to read on digital devices include computers and tablets. Liu did a research on getting people's reading habits change in the last 10 years [4]. Eighty-three percent of participants said that they increased read electronically. Similarly when students were offered to receive hard copies or read online with digital ones, Chrzastowski and Wiley found that students prefer the digital ones more [2]. Bounie and colleagues [1] also found that Amazon sells more digital books than printed books, especially in higher education [3].

In most of courses teachers usually ask students to read pieces of articles on papers or in a text as reading assignments. When students do reading activities, they make annotations on the reading materials. The annotations include notes taking and words or sentences highlighting [5]. They have their preferred ways to make annotations while reading; for instances, some of them may annotate the important words they thought in different ways (e.g., highlighting, underlining, or double-underlining).

Taking a piece of a text in the "Pollution" article[1] – "Every year in the U.S. factories release over 3 million tons of toxic chemicals into the land, air and water" – as example. When three students, John, Andrew, and Mary, see this text, John might only circle the word "air" since he feels that is the most important thing he should remember; Andrew, on the other hand, might underlines the whole sentence as he feels this information is extremely important; and, Mary, she chooses only to highlight the three words – "land", "air", and "water" – due to she believes that an item in exam may ask the destinations those toxic chemicals are released into.

First of all, they might all right about the importance of particular text or word(s), but they choose to use different way to annotate. Second, they have different perceptions toward the importance of the text and/or word(s). For example, although John and Mary have similar annotations, John either intentionally ignores or just overlooks the other words "land" and "water" while making annotations. When John is preparing an exam with the annotated article he made, he may skip those un-annotated words because he thought that he had filtered and annotated all important words or concepts already. In such case he probably will only mention "air" when he sees a question of "Environment Pollution" in the mid-term exam asking where the toxic chemicals are released to and he may lose some marks for that.

To avoid missing important thing while preparing for quizzes and exams, students usually consider to take a look at classmates' notes and even annotated texts. With such method, taking abovementioned John's case as example, he might notice that the words "land" and "water" were highlighted in Mary's text but were missed in his text. Under such circumstance, he might also consider to further circling the two words on his copy and this action may lead him to answering the question in the exam later better and getting higher marks for the exam.

The research team has designed and developed an online annotation system which acts as a platform to allow teachers creating reading activities and students doing online reading and making annotations with a variety of ways – highlight, underline, bold, italic, and the use of sidebar notes and different colours. The system also has a built-in GRACE (General Rapid Annotation Clustering Enhancement) clustering method running behind the scene to automatically group students according to their annotations [4].

With GRACE's help, the system can prompt annotation recommendations for a student immediately according to the clustering results when he or she make an annotation on the reading material. The annotation recommendations are made based on the difference among the annotations made by the students who are clustered into same group. This way, since the students in the same group are treated to have similar annotation behaviours which also implies they might have similar perceptions toward the importance of words and the passages, reminding students with the annotations

---

[1] http://webpage.pace.edu/jb44525n/page5.html

that others in the same group made may help them review and notice the potential information they overlooked or considered less important.

The paper is organized in the following way. Sections 2 and 3 use cases and screenshots to explain how teachers and students can use the online annotation system for their reading activities in their course. Section 4 makes conclusion and talks about next steps.

2 How Teachers Use the Online Annotation System

The online annotation system and its features can be seen online2. Both of teachers and students now are allowed to self-register an account and use the system. As soon as teachers register an account and sign in the system, they can create and manage their own courses freely as Fig. 1 shows. When they create a course, they need to enter a variety of information about the course – course year, season/semester/term, number, and name. They may also click "Choose" link to enter particular course to manage reading activities and review their students' annotations. They may always switch to another course by clicking "Choose a course" link at left hand side menu shown in Fig. 2.

A course can have many reading activities and teachers may setup starting and ending dates for a reading activity. Taking Fig. 2 as example, teachers can initiate the reading activity creation process by clicking "Creating reading activities" at left hand side menu. They then need to enter the reading activity's name, start and end dates, as well as the text for reading. At bottom of the reading activity creation page, a check box "No suggestion" allows teachers to decide whether or not the activity is going to provide students annotation recommendations while reading. If they think it is a good idea for their students to simply read alone, then they can choose to check this box.

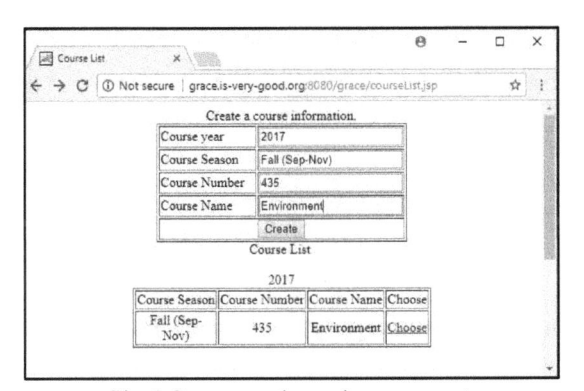

Fig. 1 Course creation and management.

---

[2] http://grace.is-very-good.org

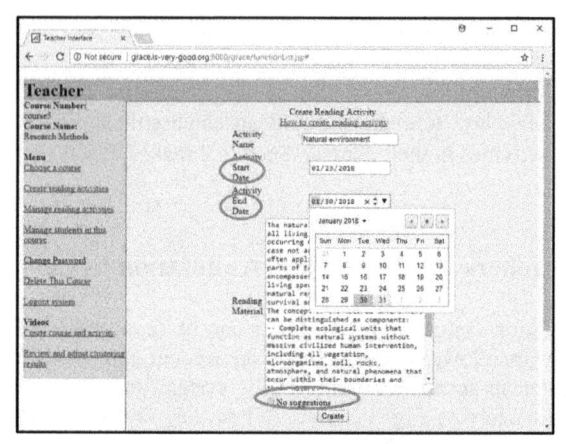

Fig. 2 Reading activity creation.

Teachers can then see and manage all reading activities they created for a course by clicking "Manage reading activities" link at the menu as Fig. 3 shows. From the list of reading activities, they can not only update and delete a reading activity but also review the annotations their students have made so far. Teachers may see the computerized clustering results or manually group students according to their wish.

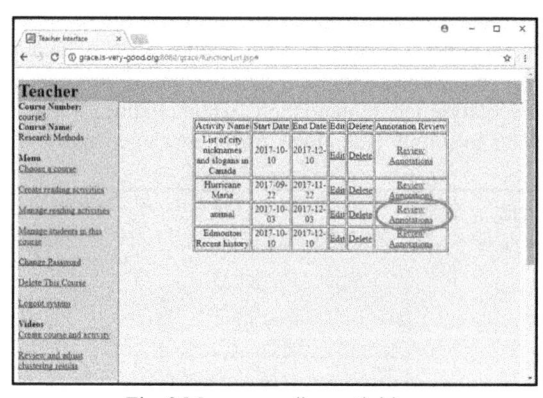

Fig. 3 Manage reading activities.

3   How Students Make Annotations and See Recommendations

When students register an account and sign in the system, they can see all courses in the system and enroll the courses they like. As soon as they enroll a course, they can check out what reading activities teachers created as Fig. 4 shows. They can start to do a reading activity by clicking "Reading" link when the activity is available – the day is between the start and end dates.

Annotation Recommendation for Online Reading Activities 139

Fig. 4 List of reading activities

Fig. 5 shows the user interface that students are reading and making annotations. They can choose single or multiple ways for making annotations, for instance, if they want to use green colour and bold font to annotate a passage, then they need to select "Multiple choice" option instead of "Single choose". When they annotate the word "wheelbarrow" on the text, the system automatically remind them to take a look back to see if they overlook "chemicals and wastes into" and may want to annotate it. If they think the recommendation is not useful, they can choose to click "Close" button to dismiss the recommendation. Students can also feel free to check "Hiding suggestions" to tell the system not giving them recommendation and avoid interruptions while reading.

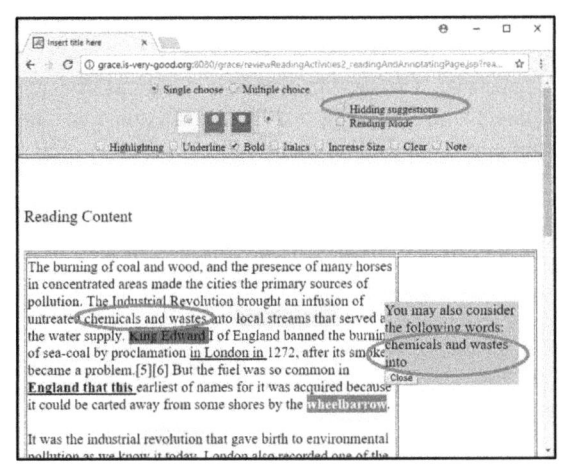

Fig. 5 Making annotations and receiving recommendation

4 Conclusion

The research team has designed and developed an online annotation system which allows teachers to create reading activities for their students and provides students annotation recommendations according their annotation similarity compared with their classmates. This paper explains how teachers and students can use the system. The next steps for the research team include (1) conducting pilots and experiments to know whether or not the system can really help teachers to know their students learning problems and how students perceived the usability toward the system; (2) providing alternative annotation recommendation mechanism which gives students recommendations about annotations made from students who are not in the same group – heterogeneous recommendation. The rationale of having heterogeneous recommendation is because sometimes "thinking out of the box" may help students learn better.

Reference

[1] Bounie, D., Eang, B., Sirbu, M., Waelbroeck, P.: Superstars and outsiders in online markets: An empirical analysis of electronic books. Electronic Commerce Research and Applications, 12(1), 52-59 (2013).
[2] Chrzastowski, T. E., Wiley, L. N.: E-book Use and Value in the Humanities: Scholars' Practices and Expectations. Library Resources & Technical Services, 59(4), 172-186 (2015).
[3] Lopatovska, I., Slater, A., Bronner, C., El Mimouni, H., Lange, L., Ludas Orlofsky, V.: In transition: academic e-book reading in an institution without e-books. Library Review, 63(4/5), 261-275 (2014).
[4] Liu, Z.: Reading behavior in the digital environment: Changes in reading behavior over the past ten years. Journal of documentation, 61(6), 700-712 (2005).
[5] Tashman, C. S., Edwards, W. K.: Active reading and its discontents: the situations, problems and ideas of readers. In SIGCHI Conference on Human Factors in Computing Systems, pp. 2927-2936. ACM (2011).
[6] Chang, M.-H., Kuo, R., Chang, M., Kinshuk, Kung, H.-Y.: Online Annotation System and Student Clustering Platform. In 8th International Conference on Ubi-Media Computing, pp. 202-207, IEEE (2015).

Big Data Analytics and Smart Service Tool: "Smart Learning Partner" Platform

Xiaoqing Li, Linghong Du, Xuanwei MA

Advanced Innovation Center for Future Education, Beijing Normal University, China
lixiaoqing8507@bnu.edu.cn, linghongdu@bnu.edu.cn, xuanweima@bnu.edu.cn

Abstract. In order to collect students' big data during learning process, model their knowledge and capability structures, and provide the individualized service based on the data, *Advanced Innovation Center for Future Education* of Beijing Normal University has researched and developed a big data analytics and smart service platform, Smart Learning Partner (SLP). This paper introduces and analyzes the SLP platform and its representative characteristics as well as explains the hidden logic of its smart service, thereby providing a reference for educators to draw upon when carrying out personalized research.

Keywords: Smart Learning Partner (SLP), big data, smart service

1 Introduction

As the National Education Reform has been further carried out, school education reform focuses more on students' competence development and the individualized service when learning behavior has done. All students aspire to obtain personalized service and smart service in the era of big data. In this sense, how to evaluate student's competence based upon their score has become a hot topic for discussion. Big data thus will gradually play a key role in providing students with smart service.

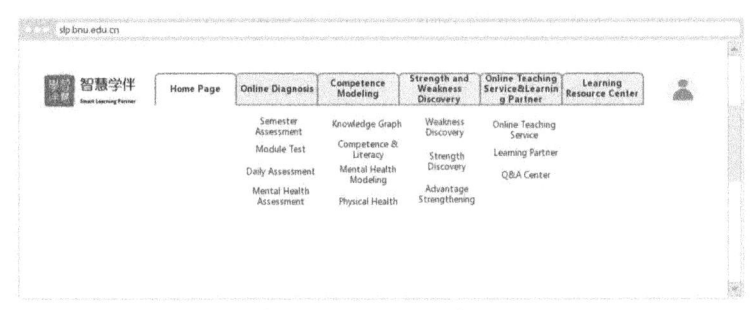

Fig.1 A prototype of SLP

"Smart Learning Partner" (SLP), an intelligent platform based on data mining and artificial intelligence technology, is developed by *Advanced Innovation Center for Future Education*, with an aim to discover and strengthen students' discipline strengths, diagnose their learning difficulties and help them address those difficulties by offering education service to elementary and middle school students, such as online assessment, personalized diagnosis report and learning resources.

2 The personalization and precision of the analysis framework

To better provide personalized service, the Research and Development (R&D) team at the Center invited experts from each discipline to discuss the operation logic between discipline competence and implementation of technology, and proposed an analysis framework based on discipline competence, which laid a foundation for the follow-up precision service. The Curriculum and Teaching Methodology professionals at Beijing Normal University have researched and developed the 3*3 Analysis Framework for Discipline Competence (3*3 Framework). 3*3 Framework is designed in hierarchy from the bottom level, learning and understanding, to the upper, practice and application and then to the top, relating and creation. The professionals also designed nine specific frameworks for each discipline according to their discipline characteristics on the basis of the original 3*3 Framework (Table 1).

Table 1. 3*3 Analysis Framework for Discipline Competence (3*3 Framework) [1].

Discipline	Three levels of discipline competence		
	A. Learning and understanding	B. Practice and application	C. Relating and creation
History	A1 Memory	B1 Explain	C1 Narration
	A2 Summary	B2 Deduction	C2 Discussion
	A3 Illustration	B3 Evaluation	C3 Exploration
Geography	A1 Observation and memory	B1 Interpretation and practice	C1 Relating and exploration
	A2 Comparison and association	B2 Calculation and skill	C2 Regional judgment and positioning
	A3 Generalization and induction	B3 Synthesis and reasoning	C3 Evaluation and planning
Chinese	……	……	……
Mathematics	……	……	……
……	……	……	……

3 Smart Learning Partner (SLP)

3.1 Collect students' big data during learning process

The premise of smart service is gathering more students' data, and the personalization of the service can only come true based on big data. The development of SLP platform is supported by data collection in three ways, including the digitized offline assessment data, the teaching and learning data, and the regular data collection of personal information. The digitized offline data refers to students' mid-term and final exams and scores produced by high-speed scanners and scoring system. The original data will be uploaded according to the 3*3 Framework to generate digitalized data. The mobile teaching and learning data refers to the data collected from mobile teaching and students' test taking and online learning using mobile terminals, during which the data can be generated naturally. The personal data collection mainly includes personal information, family background information and learning activities, which will pave the way for the follow-up analysis.

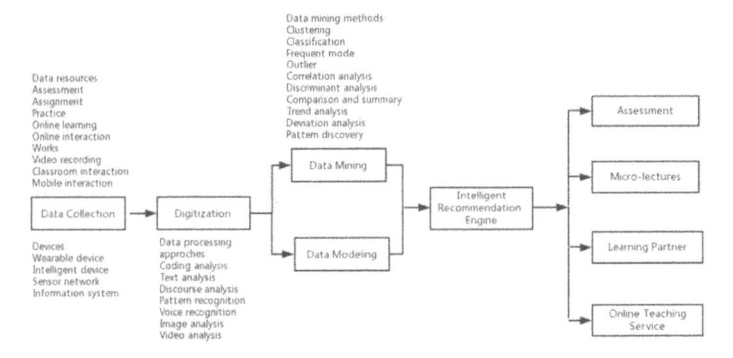

Fig.2 SLP data collection and analysis framework

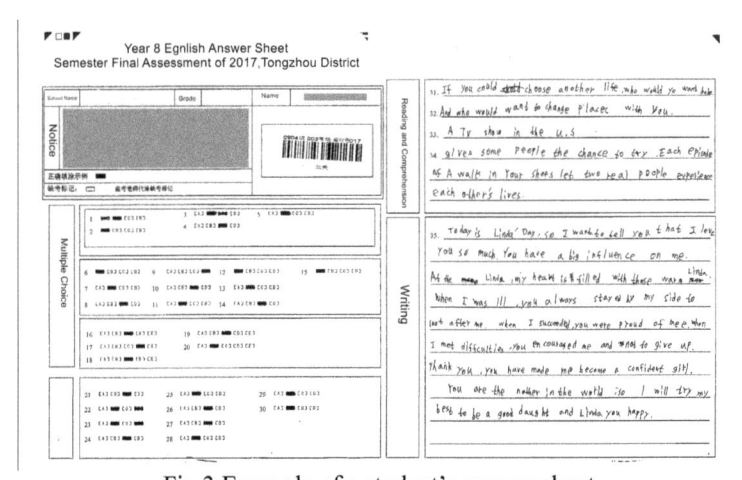

Fig.3 Example of a student's answer sheet

3.2 Generate personalized knowledge graph and competency analysis report

After collecting all kinds of students' data, data mining technology is employed to decode the data, and produce personalized reports and knowledge graphs accordingly. The personalized report refers to a specific feedback to a student after s/he took the assessment. The report is generated after decoding various data covering academic performance, discipline competence, academic achievement etc. The report varies according to the performance of students showed when completing learning tasks. A screenshot of an individual student's report in Tongzhou district is presented below.

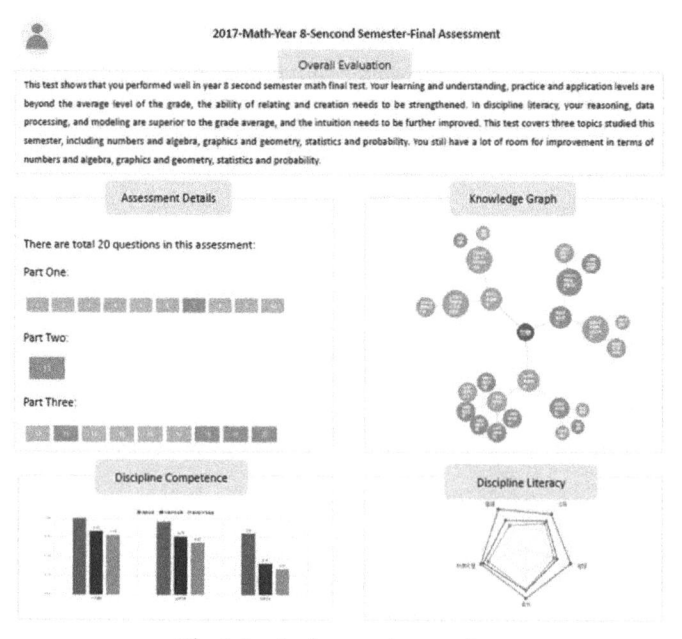

Fig.4 Analysis report example

As more learning data generated when students using SLP, algorithm analysis will be carried out to visualize students' learning process and situation of each knowledge concept, which will be shown in the form of a knowledge graph.

3.3 Provide personalized learning resources based on big data

Students' discipline strengths and weaknesses can be visualized after taking many tests. According to students' learning behavior data, the implicit correlation will be discovered to precisely predict the learning path of the students before providing them with more targeted learning resources. The personalized resources include micro-lectures covering core knowledge concepts for each discipline, and are recommended in accordance with the differences of each individual's knowledge graph.

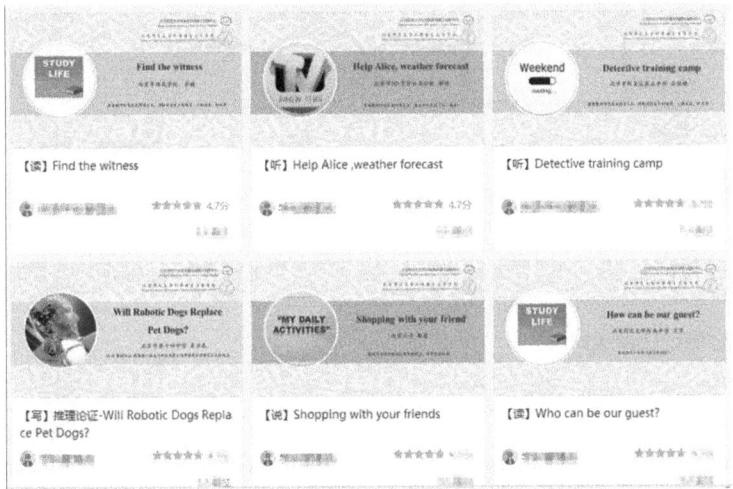

Fig.5 Recommended resources for students to learn

3.4 Provide online one-to-one teaching service based on big data

SLP provides personalized online teaching service based upon the 3*3 Framework. To accurately meet students' needs, teachers' advantages are tagged online in reference to the core concepts and 3*3 Framework, so that students can find the teacher according to their knowledge structure and competence. Online-and-offline teaching service refers to the practice that a student can obtain face-to-face teaching at school, and access to real-time tutoring online. The online teachers are recommended based on students' specific situation and diagnosis report to help them solve problems and make better achievement. This service has been done two round pilot study in Tongzhou District of Beijing, and most participant students gave positive feedback after enjoying the service. [2]

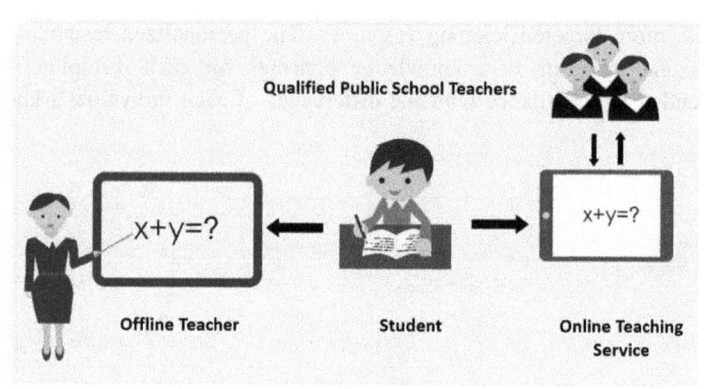

Fig.6 Online-and-offline Teaching Service

4 Conclusion

SLP is a platform with an aim to provide personalized education service based on big data analysis. To date, this platform has been widely used in Tongzhou and Fangshan districts, Beijing, with 77 schools and around 30,000 students and teachers participated in. The use of the platform will be gradually expanded to different districts of Beijing in the near future. As the research goes further, SLP added the user accounts for teachers, room teachers and principals, in support of more educators to carry out work based on big data. SLP will be further explored to generate more precise and scientific diagnosis reports and offer more innovative personalized service to students. To create a promising future for smart education service, it is highly appreciated that more educators and stakeholders can join the team to do more research and development.

References

[1] Wang, L. (2016). Exploring the Structure and Performance of Discipline Competence—Based on the Multi-dimensional Model of "Learning-Applying-Innovating". *Educational Research*, 09, 83-92+125.
[2] Chen L., Yu S. q., & Yang D. (2017). A New Exploration of the Public Service Model of Personalized Education—The Implementation of "Online-and-Offline Teacher Service". *China Educational Technology*, 07, 2-8.

[December 31, 2017]